PERSONAL CHARACTERISTICS

FROM

FRENCH HISTORY

BY

BARON FERDINAND ROTHSCHILD, M.P.

WITH PORTRAITS

London

MACMILLAN AND CO., Ltd.

NEW YORK: MACMILLAN & CO.

1896

Saint Louis.

CONTENTS

ERRATUM

P. 84, in margin, *for* Jean Vaubernier, etc., *read* Jeanne Vaubernier, etc.

LIST OF ILLUSTRATIONS

PERSONAL CHARACTERISTICS
FROM FRENCH HISTORY

THE personal characteristics of those who have
played a great, or even merely an interesting
part in the annals of the past, continue to exercise an increasing fascination over the minds
of the present generation.   Their achievements
in the various branches of human effort constitute the more important aspects of history,
but the things they said, their typical peculi-
arities of thought or action, give a more direct
clue to their personalities, and a more vivid
insight into their thoughts.   In the following
pages an endeavour has been made to present,
chiefly through the medium of their spoken
replies, an idea, however superficial, of some of
the salient characteristics of certain notable
actors in the drama of French history.   These
replies are occasionally accompanied by short
biographical sketches of the personages from
whom they proceeded, so as to obviate, as far
as possible, the compilation of a bald catalogue.
The old chroniclers of France record but few

such characteristic replies by the prominent personages of that country.   From the reign of Hugues Capet to that of Louis XIV., a lapse of several centuries, France was almost always engaged in warfare or was rent by civil strife, and the roughness of camp-life, as well as the crude customs of the day, may account for the comparative scarcity of those crisp or pregnant sayings of which later times give us so many examples.   Perhaps even a more cogent reason existed in the condition of the language, which only attained its present precision and lucidity towards the beginning of the seventeenth century, when after the wars of the League and the Fronde, and the destruction of the feudal system, France secured her homogeneity and internal peace.   The language was then recast on the basis of an imperatively strict grammar, with clearly defined rules, which facilitated a concise and epigrammatic form of expression.

Moreover, about the time when Richelieu founded the French Academy there was a general revival of letters, and the most brilliant and refined society the world has ever known then grew into being ; the most exclusive in the maintenance of social privileges and etiquette, but the most enlightened in its relations with all who had any title to distinction, to whatever class they belonged.   That society being highly trained in grace and polish of style and in the cultivation of conversational powers, took no little pride in the exquisite perfection of its diction, and set an exaggerated value on the neat modelling of a phrase. A pungent remark or a happy retort was almost sufficient to make a reputation, being eagerly taken up, repeated to a wider circle, and committed to fame by contemporary writers.

The authenticity of the sayings that have reached us from the earlier epochs has, as a matter of course, been impugned. In these days when our most cherished historical beliefs are subjected to incredulous analysis and unsparing criticism, when Tiberius is proclaimed a martyr, Bacon is asserted to have written Shakespeare's plays, and Newton declared to have discovered the law of gravitation without the descent on his brow of the famous apple, it is not, perhaps, surprising that stories handed down to us from a dim and distant past should meet with irreverent doubt. That the not too conscientious chronicler may have introduced some improvement of form in order to impart an additional piquancy to a saying, or that the historian has turned a happy idea, clumsily expressed, into a compact phrase, may be regarded as possible, or even probable, in many cases. But there need be no great scruple about accepting such phrases, and it may be taken that if the wording has been improved the sense of the original reply remains.

THE MIDDLE AGES

THE best - known reply recorded by ancient writers affords a striking example of the independent spirit of the great feudal chieftains of the early middle ages. In 987, on the death of Louis V., the last sovereign of the Carlovingian line, Hugues Capet, Duc de France and Comte de Paris, was proclaimed king at a meeting of his vassals, the great barons of the land. During his short reign he had to contend with the constant insubordination of the feudatory chiefs. 'Who made you a Count?' he said one day, turning on the Comte de Perigord, the most powerful and unruly of the nobles. 'And who made you a King?' was the bold reply.

Hugues Capet, †996.

Louis VI., le Gros, barely escaped being taken prisoner in one of his many battles with his rebellious barons. A soldier seized hold of the bridle of his horse, calling out, 'the King is taken!' 'Know, sirrah, that the King is never taken, even in chess?' replied the King, as he cut down the man with his sword. On his deathbed he sent for his son, and said to him,

Louis VI., le Gros, 1078-1137.

'Remember, my son, and keep it always before your mind, that the authority of the King is a responsibility, for which you will have to give an account on your death.'

Philippe II., called 'Auguste,' because he was born in the month of August, reigned over France in 1208. He was the friend and companion in arms of Richard Cœur de Lion, but he quarrelled with King John, wrested Normandy from the English Crown, and gradually dispossessed the Plantagenets of every inch of French soil. On the morning of the battle of Bouvines Philippe ordered mass to be said before his whole army. He placed his crown on the altar, called his generals together, and said to them, ' Here is my crown ; if one of you deems himself worthier than I am to reign over these good people, let him take it. If not, let us march on the enemy.' The King fought like any ordinary knight, but though he was thrown from his horse and trampled under foot, in the end he gained the day, defeating the Emperor of Germany and his allies, and winning the first place among the princes of Europe.

Philippe II., 1165-1223.

Simon, Comte de Montfort and Leicester, subsequently Comte de Toulouse, one of the greatest chieftains of the age, took part in the third crusade in 1202, afterwards served under the King of Hungary, and fought for five years in the Holy Land, earning high fame for valour. In 1208 he became one of the leaders of a band

Simon de Montfort, 1150-1218.

of French knights who had pledged themselves to subdue the heretical inhabitants of the south of France.   All attempts at persuasion and conciliation having failed, they proceeded to restore them to the creed of Rome by force of arms.   They besieged and, after a short resistance, took Beziers, and slaughtered indiscriminately 15,000 of its inhabitants, without any regard to whether they were Catholics or heretics.   Milon, the Papal Legate, who had been sent by Innocent III. to preach this crusade against the Albigenses, was asked by Montfort, prior to the siege, how the heretics were to be distinguished from the Catholics.   'Kill them all,' replied the envoy of the Holy Father; 'God will be able to recognise His own.'

Louis IX.,
1215-1270.
Louis IX., better known as Saint Louis, the crusader-king of France, was one of the most pious men in an age when faith was the mainspring of all actions.   He inherited his piety from his mother, Blanche of Castille, who had governed France with much ability and wisdom during his minority.   'Know, my son,' she often told him, 'that though I am devoted to you with a mother's love, I should prefer to see you dead than guilty of a mortal sin.'   In 1244 he fell dangerously ill, and pledged himself, should he recover, to join the crusades.   Four years later he sailed for Egypt, where he was successful at first, capturing Damietta, but he then fell into the hands of the

enemy. Peace was made, and the King, to regain his own liberty and that of his comrades, had to restore Damietta and pay a ransom of about seven million francs.[1] Meanwhile the Sultan of Egypt was murdered by one of his own men. The assassin, still covered with blood, rushed into the King's tent and cried out, ' How much wilt thou give me for having killed thy enemy, who would have killed thee had he lived ? ' As Louis remained silent the assassin drew his sword, pointed it at the King's breast, and said, ' Choose ! Die or make me a knight.' ' Become a Christian,' calmly replied the King, ' and I shall make thee a knight.' The man was awed, and fled.

When Philippe VI. of Valois succeeded to the throne in 1328, the Count of Flanders requested his assistance to quell an insurrection of his subjects. The King himself was inclined to comply with the request, but decided to take the opinion of his barons. The majority of the barons, when they had assembled in council, being unprepared for the expedition, recommended its postponement until the following year. The King demurred to this delay, and appealed to Gambier de Chatillon, the Great Constable of France, to support him. ' Stout hearts always find time for war,' replied Gambier, at which words Philippe embraced

Philippe VI. of Valois, 1293-1350.

---

[1] Sums of money are mentioned throughout in francs instead of livres, of which they are about the equivalent.

the Constable and exclaimed, 'Who loves me follows me!'[1]—a saying which has since become a household word in France.

Philippe VI. made a reply of singular pathos after the battle of Crécy, when, in flight before the English army, he sought refuge on a dark and stormy night at the Castle of Broye. The gates were closed, but the governor, hearing his summons, appeared on the battlements and asked, 'Who is it that calls at this hour?'

'Open!' answered the King, 'it is the fortune of France!'

The modern historical sceptic previously alluded to denies the accuracy of this version of the reply, and credits Philippe with the merely commonplace words, 'Open, open, it is the unfortunate King of France!'

Jean II., the Good, 1319-1364.

Jean II., 'the Good,' lost the battle of Poictiers to the Black Prince in 1356, ten years after his father, Philippe VI., had been defeated at Crécy. On the eve of one of the many engagements between the French and the English armies, the King in his tent heard his soldiers, as was their custom, singing the Song of Roland. 'Ah!' he exclaimed sorrowfully, 'our army has long been without a Roland.' 'There would be no lack of Rolands,' replied an old captain, who felt hurt at a remark that reflected discredit on the French arms, 'had the soldiers a Charlemagne at their head.' The King was taken

[1] 'Qui m'aime me suive.'

prisoner at Poictiers, and regained his liberty under the Treaty of Bretigny on condition of leaving his son as a hostage in England. But the young Prince made his escape, and Jean returned into captivity, saying, 'If good faith is to be banished from earth it must find a home in the hearts of kings.' The fascinations of a fair British dame, however, are supposed to have prompted this noble resolve on the part of the King as much as his good faith.

Charles V., 'The Wise,' son of Jean II., acted as Regent while his father was a prisoner in England. He got rid, for the time being, of the Grand Companies by sending them into Spain, and was distinguished for his beneficent administration of public affairs. He built the Bastille, began the Louvre, and formed a wonderful library as well as a collection of plate and works of art. The Sieur de la Rivière, his favourite, was once extolling the happiness of wielding the supreme power, when Charles observed, 'Kings are happy only in having the power to do good.' *Charles V., 1337-1380.*

Etienne Vignolles, called 'La Hire,' from *ira*, the comrade of Joan of Arc, was a typical condottiere of the Middle Ages, knowing no law or creed but that of the sword. Though no better than a bandit, La Hire's quaint humour made him a popular hero. On being reproved for the cruelties he had perpetrated, *La Hire, 1390-1443.*

he answered, 'If the Lord Himself became a gendarme, even He would turn a marauder.'

When proceeding to the siege of Montargis in 1427 he met a chaplain on the road, of whom he begged absolution. The priest having asked him to confess, La Hire said he had no time for confession, but declared that he had done what all soldiers were in the habit of doing. The priest gave him absolution, whereupon La Hire fell on his knees and uttered the supplication, 'O God, pray do for La Hire to-day what Thou wouldst La Hire would do for Thee, if he were God and Thou wert La Hire!'

Louis XI.,
1423-1483.
Louis XI., the king who first sapped the power of the great feudal barons, was as superstitious and devout as he was cunning and treacherous. An astrologer had predicted that a lady to whom he was devoted would die within a year—a prediction which happened to be fulfilled. The King ordered the astrologer to his presence, and arranged that at a given signal he should be taken hold of by his servants and thrown out of the window. When he arrived the King said to him, 'You pretend to be very clever, and to be able to foretell the fate of others. Now tell me your own fate, and how much longer you have to live.' The astrologer had either received a warning, or suspected the King's purpose, for he replied calmly, 'I shall die three days before your Majesty.' The signal was not given for his murder, and not

Louis 11.

only was he allowed to depart alive, but was afterwards treated with the greatest care and attention.[1]

One of the Ministers of Louis XI., who had been known for his peculations and extortions, had richly endowed a hospital. His munificence was mentioned admiringly to the King, but his sarcastic comment was, ' He only did what he should. Having made so many people poor in his lifetime, it was but fair that he should provide them with lodgings after his death.'

Louis XI. occasionally invited to dinner a rich and clever tradesman, who went by the name of Maitre Jean. Taking the King's kindness and condescension for more than they meant, he begged Louis XI. to grant him a patent of nobility. The King acceded to his request, but when next Maitre Jean appeared at Court to express his gratitude, he was surprised at his cool reception, and complained that he no longer got the same welcome as of old. But the King said, ' When I called you up to my table you were the first of your own order ; now that you have become the last of another, I should be insulting it were I to show you the same favour as before.'

When Louis was seized with mortal illness, and all other means had failed to restore him to health, he sent to Italy for St. Francis of Paola, *St. Francis of Paola, 1416-1507.*

[1] There is another version of this anecdote, of which the King's doctor is made the hero.

the founder of the Order of Minims, the fame
of whose great sanctity had reached him.   He
obeyed the summons of King Louis, and
remained in France until his death.   'Cure me,
holy man!   I beg of you to cure me,' implored
the moribund king.   'The Almighty,' replied
St. Francis, 'has not given me so great a power;
all I can do for you is to send up to Him the
prayers of a humble servant of God.'

A lady once consulted St. Francis on the
morality of using rouge.   'Oh!' replied the
saint, who was not versed in the arts of coquetry,
'some pious men have censured its use, some
have tolerated it.   Let us arrange a compromise
—apply rouge to one cheek only.'

THE SIXTEENTH CENTURY

Louis XII., le Père du Peuple, succeeded Charles VIII., the son of Louis XI., in 1498. During the minority of his predecessor, while Duc d'Orleans, he had led a rebellion against the Regent, Anne Beaujeu, the elder sister of Charles VIII., and so provoked the so-called *guerre folle.* He was defeated at the battle of St. Aubin by the Sire de la Tremouille, who kept him in strict confinement for some time. On ascending the throne he was advised to revenge himself on La Tremouille for the indignity he had suffered at his hands. 'It would be neither decent nor honourable for a king of France,' he replied, 'to avenge an injury done to the Duke of Orleans.'

After the battle of Agnadel (1509) Louis received, with all the honours due to his rank, Alviano, the Venetian general, whom he had beaten and taken prisoner. Alviano in return showed an ill-timed and insolent pride, whereupon the King sent him back to the camp, saying, 'Let him go! I should lose control over myself, and should regret it. I have conquered him—I must conquer myself.'

By the marriage of his daughter Claude, who was the offspring of his union with Anne, the widow of Charles VIII., the province of Brittany was secured to the French Crown. After Anne's death, though broken in health, he married Mary Tudor, sister of Henry VIII., and died within a month of his nuptials. He endeared himself to his subjects by his care for their welfare and his economy of the public finances, and many of his sayings prove the equity of his mind. 'A good king,' he said, 'is a stingy king, but I prefer to be sneered at by my courtiers for my parsimony than to oppress the people.' He died on the 1st of January, and his last words to his Consort were, 'Mignonne, I offer you my death as a New Year's gift.' His 'Mignonne' took him at his word, and was united at once to the Duke of Suffolk.

Francis I., 1494-1547. No prince could have been better suited than Francis I. to succeed his kinsman, Louis XII., during the hallowed period of the Renaissance. One of the most gallant and chivalrous sovereigns in the history of France, combining in a marked degree the characteristics of his race, he possessed the manliness and grace, the culture, refinement, and romantic love of adventure, the taste for artistic pomp and the passion for arms which were the distinguishing features of his time.

François 1.

Titian and Clouet represent Francis as tall, well-proportioned, and handsome ; his contemporaries extolled the winsomeness of his smile and the brilliancy of his blue eyes. English and Italian chroniclers, however, give a less flattering idea of his appearance. Edward Hall said of him that he was 'an attractive prince, with a proud bearing and lively manners, a dark complexion, large eyes, a long nose, thick lips, a broad chest and shoulders, short legs, and large feet.' Pasqualino, who saw Francis at Bologna, recounts a conversation he had with Henry VIII. respecting his French cousin. 'His Majesty came to me,' he says, 'and asked, " Is the King of France as tall as I am ? " I told him he was not. " Is he as stout ? " I told him he was not. " What sort of legs has he ? " I replied, "Spare." Whereupon he opened his doublet and, placing his hand on his hip, said, "Look here ! I have a good calf to my leg."'

Francis was a keen sportsman in his youth, and gave early promise of boldness above the common. It is related that while staying at Amboise he ordered a wild boar, which had been caught in the forest, to be turned out in the courtyard of the castle. The beast got loose and broke into the apartments, scattering their inmates in all directions. Francis started in pursuit alone, and killed the boar with his sword.

As soon as he ascended the throne Francis sought a wider field for his valour and ambition, and he crossed the Alps with an army of 60,000 men to wrest the Duchy of Milan from Duke Maximilian Sforza. He won the battle of Marignan, where he covered himself with glory. 'The old Marshal Trivulzio, who had accused him of lying in bed too late and of wasting his time in his mother's chamber, admitted that the battle had been fought not by men but by giants, and that the eighteen battles at which he had been present were no more than the squabbles of little children in comparison with this one.' [1]

Francis was not content with having acquired the Duchy of Milan, but aspired to possess himself of the kingdom of Naples, which then belonged to Spain. However, shortly after the battle of Marignan the old King of Spain, 'Ferdinand the Catholic,' died, and was succeeded by his grandson, the young Archduke Charles of Austria, one of the craftiest statesmen and most ambitious princes in history. In the Archduke Charles, Francis found his match, and on that day the struggle for European supremacy began between France and Austria which was destined to last for several centuries. The Imperial crown fell vacant in 1519 on the death of Maximilian I., and both Francis and Charles came forward as claimants for it. 'I shall spend three millions to be elected Emperor, and I swear that three years after my election I

[1] 'The Reign of Henry VIII.,' by G. S. Brewer.

shall either be dead or at Constantinople,' arrogantly announced Francis, who was elated by his success at Marignan and by the popularity it had brought him. But despite the millions he spent in bribing the German Electors, Charles, owing to his more legitimate claims, was called to the Imperial throne, and Francis I., to revenge himself, entered into negotiations with Henry VIII. for an alliance against the new Emperor, to which end he invited him to an interview. Henry accepted the offer. ' I have resolved to wear my beard until this meeting takes place, as a proof of my unabated desire for the interview,' said Henry to the envoy of Francis. ' And I protest,' said Francis on receiving this message, ' that I will never take off mine until I have seen the King of England.' The interview took place in June 1520, on the plains of Calais, and the two sovereigns displayed on the Field of the Cloth of Gold a magnificence that has remained famous. ' My good brother and cousin,' said Francis I. on meeting Henry VIII., ' I have come far and not without trouble to see you in person. I hope you will judge me as I am, namely, ready to assist you with my kingdoms and the lordships at my command.' ' It is not your kingdoms nor your various possessions that I consider,' replied Henry coldly, ' but the loyal observance of the promises contained in the treaties between you and me. My eyes have never seen a prince

c

dearer to my heart, and I have crossed the seas and the extreme frontiers of my kingdom to meet you.'

The tournaments, jousts, and banquets with which the kings entertained each other lasted over a fortnight, but their only result was the impoverishment of the French nobles, of whom it is recorded that, to impress their visitors by the splendour of their display, they 'carried their mills, their forests, and their meadows on their backs.' Henry VIII. remained neutral between Francis I. and Charles V., and the following year the war broke out again. In 1525 Francis took the field in person once more, and was defeated and made prisoner at Pavia. 'Madame,' he wrote in a long letter to his mother, 'this is to acquaint you of my misfortunes; of all things, there is left to me only my honour and my life.'[1] Francis' journey to Spain was more like a triumphal progress than the convoy of a prisoner. But he soon fell ill in his confinement at Madrid, and was made to sign a treaty with his Imperial jailer, in which he pledged himself to the most humiliating and onerous conditions. These, however, he refused to fulfil as soon as he had recovered his liberty, and he then challenged the Emperor to single combat. The challenge was accepted, but as neither of the two sovereigns

[1] This phrase has been crystallised in the popular saying, 'Tout est perdu fors l'honneur.'

really meant to cross swords, the duel never came off.

Though in large part owing to the enlightened efforts of the King, France emerged from the darkness of the Middle Ages into the light of modern civilisation, Francis neither enlarged her territory nor pacified her internal dissensions. During the thirty-two years of his reign he made no less than forty treaties of war and peace, constantly altered his policy and changed his allies, but his political rashness and lack of sound statesmanship wrecked every issue, his extravagance drained the resources of the country, and his profligacy corrupted its morals. In spite of his failures, his ardent patriotism, the wide scope of his ambition, his heroism in the field, his munificent patronage of literature, science, and art, and the fascination of his manners all contributed to win for him the affection of his people. · He built the palaces of St. Germain, Chenonceaux, Chambord, and Fontainebleau, adorned them with the choicest works of Italian and French sculptors and painters, and founded the Royal College for French Scholars. At his Court, the most brilliant in Europe, his sister Margaret, Queen of Navarre, the author of ' The Heptameron,' presided over a galaxy of accomplished and beautiful women ; Marot and Ronsard gave a hitherto unknown grace to French verse, and Rabelais a new vigour and purity to French prose. He

brought Benvenuto Cellini to Paris, where the
Italian goldsmith and sculptor executed many of
his masterpieces, though the majority of them
have unfortunately been destroyed. Among the
finest of these were twelve life-size statues in
gold of the Olympian divinities bearing torches,
which Louis XIV. turned into cash to pay his
soldiers. Among those which have been preserved is a large gold enamelled salt-cellar, now
in the Imperial Museum at Vienna. Francis
often went to Cellini's studio to see him at
work. He called once in 1540 to inspect the
model of a fountain the artist had been com-
missioned to make for the Château of Fontainebleau. The King, delighted with the model,
put his hand familiarly on Cellini's shoulder
and said, 'My friend, I do not know which of
us should be more gratified—the prince who
finds an artist so much after his heart, or the
artist who finds a prince able to afford him the
means of carrying out his noble conceptions.'
'The greater happiness,' said Cellini, 'is that of
the artist who has secured, as I have done, the
esteem of an illustrious sovereign.'   'Well,'
replied Francis, with a smile, 'let us put it that
our happiness is equal.'   In the same year
Charles V. requested permission from Francis I.
to pass through France on his way from Spain
to the revolted Netherlands.   Francis, putting
aside the recollection of what he had suffered at
the hands of the Emperor during his captivity

in Madrid after his defeat at Pavia, and ignoring all political considerations, not only acceded to the request, but received Charles V. with great splendour. The chivalrous conduct of the French sovereign gave rise to many sarcastic remarks, and his jester Triboulet (whose real name was Fevrial) availed himself of the opportunity.

'What are you doing?' inquired Francis one day, when he noticed Triboulet scribbling away on a paper.

'I am writing a name down on the Register of Fools,' answered Triboulet.

'What name?' asked the King.

'That of the Emperor Charles, who is committing the folly of entrusting himself to you by passing through your kingdom.'

'But how if I let him pass safely?'

'Then I shall substitute your name for his,' retorted Triboulet.

A great nobleman who had suffered from Triboulet's jibes threatened to have him flogged. The jester complained to the King.

'Have no fear,' Francis said, 'for if any one were bold enough to kill you I should have him hanged an hour afterwards.'

'Oh, sire!' replied Triboulet, 'would it not please your Majesty to have him hanged an hour before?'

Triboulet happened to be present at a meeting of the Council at which there was a discussion as to the road by which the French army should invade Italy. 'Gentlemen,' interrupted the jester, 'you appear to consider yourselves very wise, but you are strangely mistaken, for you have forgotten the most essential point.'

'And what is the most essential point?' queried a grave councillor.

'It is simple enough,' answered Triboulet. 'You have deliberated at great length as to the road by which you shall enter Italy, but you have never thought of the one you will take when you have to leave it again.'

Bayard, the *chevalier sans peur et sans reproche*, who conferred the honour of knighthood on Francis on the battlefield of Marignan, was the most accomplished and ideal knight-errant in the annals of chivalry. Bayard was fatally wounded during one of the many French campaigns in Italy, and was laid on the ground with his back to a tree and his face towards the foe. He was found in this condition by the Constable de Bourbon, the leader of the Imperial forces, against whom Bayard had been fighting. The Constable stopped and pityingly expressed his sympathy with Bayard in his cruel sufferings.

'Ah, Messer de Bayard,' said the Constable, 'what a sad plight I see you in, after all the good and loyal service you have rendered!'

'I am not to be pitied,' replied Bayard;

' I die doing my duty. It is you who deserve pity, who have been false to your prince, your country, and your oath.'

The Constable de Bourbon had become estranged from Francis I., partly because of his insatiable ambition, partly because of his refusal to respond to the passion of the King's mother, and he had gone over to Charles V. He was killed during the siege of Rome, three years after Bayard's death, by a shot from a cross-bow, which Benvenuto Cellini in his auto-biography boasts of having aimed. *Constable de Bourbon, 1489-1527.*

Catherine de Medicis was married to Henry II., the son of Francis I., and was the mother of the last three kings of the Valois branch of the Capet dynasty—Francis II., Charles IX., and Henry III. She ruled the country during the minority of Charles IX. and instigated the Massacre of St. Bartholomew in 1572. She is supposed to have caused the death of Jeanne d'Albret, Queen of Navarre, by pre-senting her with a pair of poisoned gloves. Jeanne d'Albret had been brought up a Catholic, but became an ardent convert to the Pro-testant faith, from which Catherine vainly endeavoured to wean her. ' Madame,' replied Jeanne d'Albret to Catherine, ' had I my kingdom and my son at hand, I would rather throw them both into the sea than go to Mass!' She soon paid the penalty for these proud words. *Catherine de Medicis, 1519-1589.*

The Italy of the sixteenth century was personified in this daughter of the Medicis. She had classical features, fair hair, a pale complexion, and blue eyes which reflected every passing emotion, but concealed her inmost thoughts. Her conversation was light, sparkling, and full of humour, and in her earliest years she astonished the Court by her capacity for appreciating the grave political problems of the time. She was fond of reading and hunting, invented the pommel for the side-saddle, patronised artists, and built the palace of the Tuileries; and though she was vain, and encouraged the intrigues of her ladies in order to utilise them as a means of discovering the political secrets of her enemies, she was a dutiful wife and a devoted mother. A bigoted adherent to the faith of her ancestors, still she was altogether in the hands of Ruggieri, a Florentine astrologer, whom she advanced to high ecclesiastical honours; and while cold and cruel towards political adversaries, personal affronts failed to affect her. One day, on hearing a song in which she was grossly insulted, she only laughed, and prevented the King of Navarre from seizing and hanging the culprit. 'Such a man, cousin,' she told him, 'is not big enough game for us.'

Her lot was cast in a critical time for herself, for France, and her children. The country was turned into an armed camp by political and religious feuds. The turbulent ambition of the Condés, the Duc de Guise, and of their followers threatened the throne as seriously as the growing power of the Protestant leaders did the supremacy of the Roman Catholic Church. Fortune alternately favoured the Catholic and the Protestant cause. At times it seemed as if the throne must perish ; but Catherine never lost heart, and always adapted herself to changing circumstances. After the defeat of the Royalists at the battle of Dreux in 1562 she calmly said, 'In future we shall have to hear mass in French.' But she was as deceitful as she was patient and enduring, and she bided her time. By playing off one party against the other and stimulating their rivalries she kept the throne in security between them. The Protestants were defeated at the battle of Jarnac in 1569 by her son, the Duc d'Anjou (afterwards Henry III.), and their commander, the Prince de Condé, was murdered. But Charles IX. was jealous of Anjou, and either to spite him or his mother, or from a genuine change of feeling, he took Coligny, the Protestant leader, into favour.

The Massacre of St. Bartholomew afterwards took place, and it settled the religious question in France for ever. It would hardly be fair to fasten the crime entirely on Catherine. That she decoyed the Protestant leaders to Paris and obtained the sanction of Charles IX. to the plot to murder them can hardly be questioned ; but the general massacre that followed was, on the whole, rather the outcome of the fierce and uncontrollable passions of the dominant Catholic party. There was nothing to choose between Protestants and Catholics in their savage hatred of each other. Whenever the opportunity presented itself the Protestants butchered the Catholics; but as after St. Bartholomew the victory remained with the latter, and as a larger number of victims was then slain by them than had ever been slain by the Protestants on any previous occasion, and, moreover, as Catherine ruled at the time, and as she and her son were the chief gainers by the massacre, the whole responsibility for it has been cast on her.

Henry III.,
1551-1589.
Catherine's sons, the youngest especially, Henry III., had to contend with the ambition of the Duc de Guise, who, had he not been deficient in resolution, might at one time have succeeded in usurping the Crown. Though warned by their friends, both the Duke and his brother, the Cardinal de Lorraine, accepted an invitation to the Castle of Blois, where they were murdered by the orders of the King. Catherine was almost at death's door when the King announced the accomplishment of the deed to her.

'Madame,' he said, 'now I really am king ; I have just rid myself of the Duke of Guise.'

' It is well cut,' replied Catherine ; ' now you must stitch.'

But Henry III. stitched in vain. Though he became reconciled to Henry of Navarre (the future Henry IV.), he was assassinated a few months afterwards by Jacques Clément, a fanatical monk.

HENRI IV.

HENRI IV. was lineally descended from Robert,
Baron de Bourbon, the sixth son of St. Louis.
The branches of the Capet dynasty still bear
the title which was conferred on the prince
from whom they spring in the direct line.
The Capetiens reigned until 1328, when Charles
IV. died, leaving no male issue and no brother.
Philippe VI. became king, being descended from
Charles of Valois, the younger brother of Philippe
IV., and his successors in the direct line bore
the name of Valois until they became extinct
on the death of Henri III. The House of
Bourbon occupied the throne until 1830, when
the crown was taken by Louis Philippe, the
lineal descendant of the brother of Louis XIV.,
the Duke of Orleans ; hence his descendants
still call themselves ' Orleans.'

Henri IV. is still a popular hero in France,
and his name was long one to conjure with.
He drove the foreigner from the country,
put an end to religious and internecine strife,

Henri 4.

gave his Protestant subjects their civil and religious rights, and, with the assistance of capable Ministers, pacified and reorganised his dominions and set its finances in order. He succeeded three worthless and despicable kings, and preceded one who might have been an Italian princeling of the decadence. Henri IV. was a great sovereign, simple in private life, dignified, brave, and richly endowed with Gallic humour, eminently patriotic, full of sympathy for his people, who, on their side, admired him for his qualities as well as his foibles. His noble and picturesque figure still stands out in bold relief on the page of French history. Posterity has treasured up many of his sayings. On one of his progresses he stopped to dine at a village, and gave orders that the most intelligent man in the place should be brought up to converse with him during the meal. The rustic having made his appearance, he was directed to sit opposite the King at table.

'What is your name?' inquired Henri IV.

'Sire, I am called Gaillard.'

'What is the difference between Gaillard (a jolly fellow) and *paillard* (a rake)?'

'Sire,' was the reply, 'there is but a table between the two.'

'Ventre Saint Gris!' cried the King, laughing, 'I never thought to find so great a wit in so small a village.'

When Henri IV. entered Marseilles he was
presented with an address, which began with the
words, 'When Hannibal left Carthage.' The
King, foreseeing a long and tedious oration,
interrupted the worthy spokesman by saying,
'When Hannibal left Carthage he had dined,
so I am going to have my dinner.' At
Amiens, where he arrived after a very fatiguing
journey, he was received in the same way with
a harangue which began, 'Most great, most good,
most clement, most magnanimous——' 'And
most wearied,' added the King ; and he left.

Henri IV. was once staying at the Palace
of Fontainebleau when he noticed a labourer
named Lefoy standing on the terrace and gazing
intently at the ornamental gardens. ' What are
you looking at, my good man ? ' asked the King.
' At your gardens, sire ; they are certainly very
fine, but I have one which is far better.'
' Where is your garden ? ' asked the King.
' Near Malesherbes, sire,' answered the labourer.
' Well, I should like to see it,' rejoined the
King. Some days later Henri IV., happening
to pass through Malesherbes, asked to be shown
Lefoy's garden. The man took him to a
large cornfield which was in splendid condition.
' You are right,' said the King, ' your garden
is finer and better than mine,' and to prove how
much he valued Lefoy's husbandry, as well as
to encourage agriculture, he granted Lefoy the
privilege of wearing a gold wheat-ear in his cap.

On another occasion, returning to Paris from a hunt in the neighbourhood, he crossed the Seine in a small boat. Being plainly clad, and attended only by a couple of gentlemen, he was not recognised by the boatman, whom he asked what the people thought of the Peace of Vervins, which had just been concluded with Spain. ' Well,' said the boatman, ' I don't know much about this Peace, but what I do know is, that everything in the land is taxed — even this miserable boat, which hardly affords me a livelihood.' ' But won't the King reform the taxes?' asked Henri. ' The King is a good fellow enough, but he has mistresses who require such a lot of money, such fine gowns and trinkets, that there is no end to it, and it is we who have to pay for it all,' and then the man went on abusing the reigning favourite, Gabrielle d'Estrées. The King, who had been much amused by the man's talk, sent for him the following day, and made him repeat, in the presence of Gabrielle, what he had said the preceding evening. She, on the contrary, was highly incensed at the candour of the boatman, and wished to have him sent to the gallows. ' No,' replied Henri, ' he is only a poor devil whom poverty has soured. He shall no longer pay for his boat, and then I am sure he will shout " Vive Henri! Vive Gabrielle!"'

Throughout his life Henri Quatre was the victim of his weakness for women, and had not the knife of Ravaillac brought his career to a sudden close, he might have imperilled the peace of the country by his passion for the Princesse de Condé, whom her jealous husband had removed across the frontier. The King had selected Pierre Mathieu, a distinguished historian, to write an account of his life. When the author read to him some passages in which he alluded to the King's devotion to the fair sex, the latter asked, 'Why do you reveal my weaknesses?' 'Because,' replied Mathieu, 'they will afford as good a lesson to the Dauphin as the account of your many noble deeds.' Having pondered a while, Henri said, 'Yes, the whole truth must be told; were my defects to be ignored, other things would not be believed—well, write them down, so that I may avoid them in future.'

Henri IV. was 'clement and magnanimous,' to quote the words of the Maire of Amiens, but though he stamped out sedition, he was not able to smother treason. Charles de Gontault had been one of his most trusted followers and captains. The King made him *Duc de Biron, 1561-1602.* a marshal and Duc de Biron, and honoured him greatly. But Biron secretly plotted against the State, and entered into a conspiracy to betray the King to his enemies. Biron was one of the best tennis-players of the day, and having on one occasion particularly excelled in his play, the circumstance was reported to the King—

'Yes, but though he plays well, he is not very successful in his games,' was his remark, alluding to Biron's conspiracy. At first he pardoned his old friend, but, as Biron continued playing his 'game,' it eventually cost him his life.

A young fop of unprepossessing appearance, with whom Henri was not acquainted, had made his way into the palace. At that time the minor nobility, or the scions of great families, were attached to the suite of some illustrious nobleman, to whom, in the parlance of the day, they 'belonged.' 'To whom do you belong?' inquired the King. 'To myself,' pertly replied the young man. 'Then you have a very silly master,' rejoined the King.

Generosity was not a quality in which Henri IV. excelled, and his companions-in-arms, whom he often treated in the most niggardly fashion, made no ceremony about telling him occasionally what they thought of him on that score. One night D'Aubigné — Madame de Maintenon's grandfather — said to the Duc de la Force, who was sleeping near him in the King's closet, 'La Force, our master is the most ungrateful mortal on earth.' La Force was dozing, and asked him to repeat what he had said. 'Why, you are deaf!' unexpectedly interposed the King, who was thought to have been fast asleep; 'he says that I am the most ungrateful of all human beings.' 'Sleep, sire,

D

sleep, we have much more to tell each other,' re-joined D'Aubigné. 'Next morning,' D'Aubigné relates in his Memoirs, 'the King looked on us as kindly as ever, but he did not give us a sou the more.'

Though not an exemplary husband, Henri IV. was greatly attached to his children, and delighted in playing and romping with them. One day the Spanish Ambassador, on entering the royal closet, found the King walking on all fours carrying the Dauphin on his back. Henri IV. asked him without rising, ' M. l'Ambassadeur, have you a family?' and being answered in the affirmative, the King returned, ' Then I can finish my tour round the room.'

His most memorable words were addressed to his followers before the battle of Ivry, when he defeated the army of the League under the Duke of Mayence. 'Close up your ranks,' he told them, 'and if you lose your colours, your cornets, and your standard-bearers, rally round my white plume ; you will always find it on the road to honour and victory.'

The two best-known phrases attributed to him, however, are held by some authorities to be apocryphal :—' Paris is well worth a mass' implies a cynical levity of which Henri was not likely to have been guilty ; and ' I wish every French peasant to have a fowl in the pot' could hardly have been said at a time when a fowl was an unwonted luxury.

Cardinal Richelieu

LOUIS XIII. AND RICHELIEU

HENRI IV. had quelled the turbulence of the great feudal chiefs, but on his death, and during the minority of his son, Louis XIII., disorder broke out again. The whole of his successor's reign was a struggle for supremacy between the Crown and the nobles, which ended in the victory of the Crown, thus paving the way for the autocratic rule of Louis XIV. It may be said, indeed, that the cause of the Crown was won by a single man, Cardinal Richelieu. Originally trained for the army, he went into the Church, and at the age of twenty-two was made Bishop of Luçon. During the earlier part of his career he resided in his diocese, where he devoted himself exclusively to ecclesiastical and theological work. The Queen Regent, Marie de Medicis, appointed him her almoner ; he soon gained her favour, became a member of the King's Council, and then, with indomitable audacity and persever-ance, entered upon his task of subduing the nobility and breaking their power. 'I under-

Louis XIII., 1601-1643.

Armand du Plessis, Cardinal de Richelieu, 1585-1642.

take nothing,' he said to one of his friends,
'without mature consideration, but when I
have made up my mind, I mow down everything that stands in my way and then cover
it up with my red cassock.' His biographers
have been more intent on recording the
manner in which he 'mowed down' everything than in transmitting to us his conversational sallies, of which he must presumably
have made many, for he was a man of the
highest culture, had great literary tastes, and
in the intervals of his sanguinary conflicts was
fond of enjoying the pleasures of society, and
keenly relished a joke. One day he asked his
confessor how many masses were required to
deliver a soul from purgatory. 'It is not
known,' gravely replied the divine; 'the Church
has not specified.' 'You are an ignoramus,'
answered the Cardinal; 'as many masses are
required as snowballs to light a stove.'

Richelieu had pleasant and attractive manners,
but was hard-hearted and deceitful, and whoever
barred his way was ruthlessly removed. A
man of such grim character could not have
many friends. Yet he was true to the last
François to the comrade of his youth, Père Joseph.
Leclerc de This Capuchin friar came of a noble house,
Tremblay, and played an important part in the secret
1577-1638. history of the political and ecclesiastical affairs
of the country, for he was Richelieu's right-
hand man and confidential adviser. 'I know

no minister in Europe,' the Cardinal said of him,
'who is capable of shaving the Capuchin monk,
although there is plenty to catch hold of.'[1]
The power of the Capuchin was well known,
and while Richelieu was called 'His Red Eminence,' he was known as 'His Grey Eminence.'

It is hard to determine to what extent the
King liked his Minister. There could be
nothing in common between .two men who
were so thoroughly the antithesis of each other
in constitution and character. Richelieu was
often on the point of being disgraced, and
Louis always seemed to listen favourably to the
malicious intrigues of his enemies. Yet when
the Cardinal died Louis XIII. showed genuine
emotion. The King's health was undermined
by consumption, he was morose, incompetent,
irresolute, and suspicious ; he cared for nothing
but hawking and his pet birds, for music and
the pursuit of minor arts and trades. He was
a hopelessly weak man, left the management
of the State first to his mother, whom he afterwards banished, and then to his great Minister,
whom he feared and obeyed till they were parted
by death.

Louis XIII. in his youth was wilful and
obstinate, and one day, as he refused to say his
prayers, his mother had him whipped by his
governor, M. de Souvré. The young King

[1] 'Je ne connais pas de ministère en Europe capable
de faire la barbe à ce Capucin quoiqu'il y-ait belle prise.'

resisted for a time, but finally submitted, with the remark, 'I see it must be gone through, but, M. de Souvré, pray go gently about it.' When, next day, he called on his mother, she, according to etiquette, made him a deep curtsey. 'Oh, Madame!' he said, with a sense of humour he seldom betrayed in later life, 'pray make fewer curtseys and have me whipped less severely.'

When fourteen years old, Louis was declared of age, according to the royal custom of those days, and was married to Anne of Austria. His mother, however, still continued *Marie de* to rule in his name.   Marie de Medicis had *Medicis,* *1573-1642.* nothing in common with her illustrious relative Catherine, except an inveterate hatred of the Reformed Church.   She had been handsome in her youth, though less handsome than she was represented in the portraits that had been sent from Florence when she was betrothed to Henri IV., for whom she cared as little as he cared for her.   Poor in spirit, obstinate, and ill-tempered, she had no ideas of her own, and borrowed her policy from her Ministers and favourites. Concini, the son of a Florentine lawyer, a dissolute but ambitious youth, insinuated himself into her good graces, married her maid Eleonore Galigai, and followed her to France.   In time he rose to be First Minister of the Council, was created Marquis d'Ancre, and, though he had never drawn a sword, became a Marshal of France. Concini was soon drunk with his success.   His pride and ambition exceeded all bounds, and he aimed at founding an independent principality in the south of France. But his insolence gave general offence at Court and estranged the foreign Ambassadors. As long as Louis XIII. was only a boy, and while the country was distracted by civil war, Concini was able to play his game with impunity, but now that the King was of age, Concini should have been more careful in his proceedings. As it was, a drama was enacted in the Louvre which vividly illustrated the lawless spirit of the age and the barbarous characteristics of its chief personages.

In the same way that Marie de Medicis was influenced by Concini, Louis was governed by his favourite, Charles d'Albert, Duc de Luynes, who had won the affections of the young sovereign by his skill in training birds and his taste for falconry. De Luynes, who was as wily as the Italian, coveted his position, and stealthily set to work to alienate the King from his mother and her favourite. He told the King that his realm was in the hands of a foreigner who was universally detested ; and to excite his jealousy he dwelt on the preference shown by the Queen for her second son, Gaston, Duke of Orleans. Then Concini's consultations with astrologers were brought to the King's notice by De Luynes, who suggested that their object was to throw a spell over his royal master ; even the word poison was muttered. Louis, who was destitute

Duc de Luynes, 1578-1621.

of a spark of genuine feeling, reverence, or gratitude, eagerly listened to these insinuations, and placed himself in the hands of De Luynes. At first it was only intended to imprison Concini, but after a time the King ordered him to be murdered, and Vitry, the Captain of the Guard, was entrusted with the carrying out of the deed. The murder was fixed for Sunday, 25th April 1617. The King went to Mass, and then, with consummate duplicity, he called on and conversed with his mother, afterwards returning home to await the execution of his orders. But owing to some defect in the arrangements the attempt was not made that day. Early on the following morning the King made preparations as if to go out hunting, but instead of leaving the palace he loitered talking to De Luynes and his friends. Vitry and his men were posted in the courtyard in expectation of Concini's arrival, and horses stood ready saddled close by to aid the King's flight in case of failure. At ten o'clock Concini arrived at the Louvre attended by a large suite, and the moment he entered the courtyard Vitry touched his arm and said, ' The King has ordered me to arrest you.' ' *A me!* ' shouted Concini to his followers, seeing he had been trapped. ' Yes, to you! ' retorted the Captain, making a signal to his men, who instantly shot down Concini with pistols and then despatched him with their daggers. The deed accomplished, Vitry contemptuously spurned with his foot the body of the man who had virtually ruled France, and cried out ' Vive le Roi.' The fray had brought one of the Queen's women to the window, and hearing from Vitry that he had killed the Marshal by the King's order, she rushed to impart the information to her mistress. ' Oh me!' cried out the Queen in her anguish, ' I have reigned seven years, and now I have nothing to hope for but a crown in heaven.' She had not a word to say for her favourite's miserable end, and being asked how the news should be broken to Eleonore Galigai, she petulantly replied, ' Eh! I have other matters to consider now ; if you cannot say it to her, then sing it to her.' Then, as she paced her room wringing her hands, she kept saying, ' Do not talk to me of these people ; I warned them ; they should have gone back to Italy ; I must now think of myself.' The news was finally imparted to Eleonore Galigai by one of the Guard. ' He must have been killed by the King!' exclaimed the wretched woman, and instead of deploring the fate of her husband, she called him a lunatic, said his pride had brought him to a bad end, and busied herself secreting her jewels and money.

Throughout this ghastly drama the person-ages concerned exhibited only the lowest form of ambition and treachery and the most cynical selfishness. None of them profited in any way by their baseness. Louis soon fell under the sway of Richelieu, by whom he was more completely dominated than his mother had ever been by Concini. Marie de Medicis was exiled to Blois, and though she was shortly permitted to return to Court, the King always treated her with studied indifference. In 1631 he banished her from France, and she died, ten years later, in great distress at Cologne. De Luynes lived only a short time to enjoy the King's favour, being carried off by a fever in 1621. Eleonore Galigai was accused of sorcery and beheaded. Even Concini's remains were not allowed to rest. They had been secretly conveyed the night after his assassination to the Church of St. Germain l'Auxerrois. But the mob got wind of the fact, and, with blind rage, they disinterred the body, cut it in pieces, roasted the mutilated fragments, dragged them in triumph through the streets, and then flung them into the river.[1]

Though weak and irresolute, Louis showed some courage in the field. At the battle of Royan in 1622 a shot passed close over his head. 'Good heavens!' cried out a general at his side, 'that shot almost killed your Majesty.' 'No, not me,' replied the King, 'it was D'Epernon.' Then seeing that some of his suite were still running away, he exclaimed ironically, 'Are you afraid of this gun? Are

[1] See Hanotaux's 'Richelieu.'

you not aware that in order to be fired it must be loaded again?'

Marshal Bassompierre, one of Richelieu's many victims, had been sent to the Bastille, and only regained his liberty at that Minister's death. When he appeared at Court Louis asked him his age. Bassompierre replied that he was fifty, but the King, who knew him to be sixty, reproached him for not answering truly. 'Sire,' answered Bassompierre, 'I did not reckon the ten years I spent in the Bastille, as they were not devoted to your Majesty's service.' The courtiers were seemingly already training themselves for the flatteries they were to lavish on Louis XIV.

The King noticed one evening at a function that the courtiers crowded round the omnipotent Minister, leaving him alone and unnoticed. 'Pass on!' he angrily said to Richelieu, who stood aside to let him go by ; 'pass on, as you are the first here!' 'Yes, sire,' replied the Cardinal, taking hold of a light, 'but it is in order to show the way to your Majesty.'

Louis XIII. only survived Richelieu three months. Shortly before he died he sent for the Dauphin, and playfully asked him his name. 'I am called Louis XIV.,' said the child.

'Not yet, not yet, my boy,' murmured the moribund king.

MAZARIN

On his deathbed Richelieu bequeathed Cardinal
Mazarin to Louis XIII., and the very day after
his death the King issued an order appointing
Mazarin a member of the Council, trusting
the Cardinal from that moment as if he had
been a born Frenchman. Comparisons have
often been made between the two great men
who governed France during the first half of the
seventeenth century. The temptation to indulge
in such comparisons is obvious, though they
only help to show the wide contrast between
Richelieu and Mazarin. Both were originally
intended for the army, but both entered the
Church, and eventually wore the Red Hat of
Rome; both filled the same position at the head
of affairs for many years, and each achieved the
purpose on which his ambition was set—in the
one case the erection of France into a great power,
in the other the establishment of the autocracy of
the Crown; finally, both were patriotic to the
core, so that, though Mazarin was an Italian, and
never even mastered the language of the country

Cardinal Mazarin.

he ruled, he could well say, ' My heart is French, though my language is not.' But there the resemblance ends. Richelieu was the scion of a noble house ; Mazarin at the outset of his career was an adventurer. Richelieu had all the idiosyncrasies of a great genius ; he trampled down with indomitable energy and courage every obstacle that stood in his way. Mazarin was a courtier, a subtle and adroit diplomat, whose motto was ' Time and I,' and who sent his enemies to the Bastille instead of to the scaffold. Richelieu was successful from first to last ; Mazarin knew the bitterness of adversity. For a long time Mazarin's work was uphill, and twice he had to fly from France. This is not the place for a history of the Wars of the Fronde, of which he was the central figure, but they may be alluded to, for the reason that they were the last flickers of the flame that had wrought so much havoc in the land, the last manifestation of the spirit of opposition on the part of the nobility to the Crown — wars which were mean in their character and ignoble in their aims, for they had their origin in petty rivalries, and their object was personal aggrandisement. Moreover, the Wars of the Fronde first brought into play the direct influence of women in politics, an influence they were soon to exercise on all the relations of life. The Duchesses de Montpensier, de Longueville, de Chevreuse were not only the heroines of the Fronde, but they were the friends of the Marquises de Rambouillet, de la Fayette, and de Sévigné, to whom, as much as to La Rochefoucauld, Malesherbes, Voiture, and Pascal, the French tongue was indebted for its transformation. A new era now opened ; the rough and sinewy but picturesque expressiveness of ancient times disappeared with the doublet and hose, and instead of the quaint and forcible language of the men of blood and iron of the past, refinement of style became the mark of good breeding, and gracefully turned compliments and pointed witticisms the fashionable parlance.

'In France everything ends in a song' is an old adage, and no French public man was more virulently derided in song than Mazarin ; but these songs neither pained nor annoyed him. When he levied some additional taxes there was an abnormal explosion of satirical verse, and on this being reported to him, he placidly observed, 'They sing ; they will pay.' When in office, he was overwhelmed with petitions, but the petitioners were not always admitted to his presence. The Governor of the Bastille, however, begged him to receive a relative of his own, who merely asked the favour of saying two words. 'Be it so,' said the Cardinal, 'but mind, two words only.'

It happened to be a very cold day when the petitioner entered Mazarin's apartment. A large

fire blazed on the hearth. Looking at it, he
uttered the two words—

'Cold, hungry!'

'Fire, bread!' Mazarin answered laughing,
and ordered him a pension.

He was fond of cards, and one day a discussion arose over a game of picquet. The
Cardinal was shouting violently, while the rest
of the party looked on in silence, when the poet
Benserade chanced to come into the room, and
though he knew nothing of what had occurred,
he went up to the table and said quietly, 'Your
Eminence is wrong!'

'How can you tell?' asked the Cardinal
hotly.

'The silence of these gentlemen is the best
evidence,' replied the poet, 'for were you right
they would shout much louder than you do.'

When Mazarin was on the point of death,
Anne of Austria, to whom he was said to have
been secretly married (Mazarin had never been
ordained, and was a lay-cardinal), called to
inquire for him. 'I am very ill, madam,' he
replied, 'and see,' he added, ostentatiously dis-
playing his legs, which were withered by disease,
'see these legs! they have lost their repose in
giving it to the State.'

THE REIGN OF LOUIS XIV.

For the sake of convenience, history is usually divided into centuries, and the impression is thus created that certain historical and social commotions begin or end with arbitrary dates. But while history obeys the same laws of continuation and change as nature, and the progress of mankind does not start or stop at any particular period, the eighteenth century of France has so distinct a character of its own that it can almost be defined within two clearly ascertainable dates. It may be said to have begun with the death of Louis XIV. on 1st September 1715, and to have ended with the taking of the Bastille on 14th July 1789. The first fifteen years of the eighteenth century belonged in effect to the preceding century, while the Revolution, its most momentous event, though it began eleven years before the close of the eighteenth, virtually belonged to the nineteenth century. The seventeenth century may be divided into various chapters, which may be severally assigned to Henri IV., Richelieu, Mazarin, and

Louis 14.

Louis XIV.; so that it dovetails into the eighteenth. The French, who have eminently logical minds, usually speak of 'the century of Louis XIV.,' but to be hypercritically accurate, only half of it can rightly be claimed for him, as he did not begin to govern personally until 1661, though his supreme individuality dominated a long period, during which he overshadowed his contemporaries. It seems almost strange that this should be so. He was in many ways an ignorant and ill-educated man. But nevertheless he was eminently a leader of men, and though he ruled far from wisely, or even well, he understood the temperament of his subjects, and governed them with masterful force.

Louis XIV., 1638-1715.

Louis XIV. inherited none of the salient characteristics either of his father or grandfather; he possessed neither the moroseness and weakness of Louis XIII. nor the humour and bravery of Henri IV., but he had all the Austrian pride of his mother. He was fond of society, of pomp, and of intercourse with clever men, but his own conversational gifts were limited. War occupied a great part of his prolonged reign. He was present at many battles and sieges, but it was always arranged that he only arrived at a siege when it was about to end; while, on the battlefield, he was invariably placed in a secure position. All his ideas and conceptions were lofty. He was

E

ambitious, it is true, and raised France to an undreamt - of position of greatness, but his ambition was personal rather than patriotic. 'When one works for the State, one is working for oneself,' were his own words. For his wife, his Ministers, and his people he never showed any consideration. Probably he was religious ; he was certainly bigoted, and attended divine service regularly, but his humility before God was of a cheap kind. The God he worshipped was far away in heaven, and not in his heart or on earth, where he would brook no rival. He was the sole fountain of honour ; the highest dignitaries of the Church trembled at his frown. Whether owing to his ailments or to his pride, he was choleric, and but for the intervention of Madame de Maintenon, he would on one occasion have caned the Duc de Lauzun, while on several others he made a sorry exhibition of himself. As he grew older he suffered from gout and rheumatism, and was always in the hands of his doctors, and that, in spite of their remedies, he lived to a great age attests the robustness of his constitution. It was his constant aim from first to last to give an overpowering impression of dignity, even in the smallest matters. His baldness compelled him to wear a wig, and he was most careful never to be seen without it, even by his servants. It was handed to him through the curtains of his bed before he rose, and he handed it back in the same manner to his attendants at night. His stature being short, he invented high-heeled shoes to remedy the remissness of nature. For the same reason he was careful neither to offend his courtiers nor elate them unduly by some rashly-spoken word. In his youth he was very handsome, and fascinated the people; but he was devoid even of those passions which in one of his station may be taken for genuine emotion.

Egotism was his cardinal failing; crass egotism, selfishness, and heartlessness pervaded his public career and turned his heart to stone. These defects were exhibited in his relations with women more than in any other way. He never showed any real affection to the women he loved, or fancied he loved, or evinced any gratitude for their devotion. When their part was played out he cast them off like an old coat.

Louis XIV. happened to live at a time of transition, when the old order was giving place to the new. The upper classes had been crushed into subjection by the iron hand of Richelieu, and the vitality of the people, which had been diverted into stray channels during his long minority by the troubles of the Fronde, expanded with unwonted vigour and luxuriance. No monarch was ever better served by circumstances. France never had a more brilliant host of generals, men of letters, and artists, and he had the good policy to patronise and encourage their efforts, although his egotism always enabled him to utilise these efforts for his own glorification. In his old age, when the country had been ruined by his selfish extravagance and ambitious crazes, his generals were beaten, and literature and art assumed a different complexion, and adapted themselves to a different age. He was certainly a great king, and had he died in 1685, before the Revocation of the Edict of Nantes and the War of Succession, his fame as a ruler would have been unblemished, and he would have handed down to his successor a priceless inheritance. But he survived both himself and his time. For the great achievements of those early halcyon days of his reign the credit was not altogether his.

Though chary of blame or of praise, Louis XIV. could effectively bestow either when the occasion demanded. A young fop who was jealous of an old courtier said in the King's hearing that quite a large book could be written on the subjects of which the courtier in question was ignorant, whereupon the King sternly retorted, 'And a very small one could be written on those of which you know anything.'

Prince de Condé, 1621-1686. After the victory of Sénef in 1674, the Great Condé was received by the King at the head of the grand staircase at Versailles, which the Prince, who was suffering from gout, had some difficulty in ascending, so he said apologetically, 'Sire, I beg your Majesty's pardon for keeping you waiting.' 'Do not hurry, cousin,' replied the King; 'when one is weighted with laurels as you are, one could not proceed any faster.'

One day the Prince de Condé complained of the noise made by the young Duc du Maine, the son of Louis XIV. and Madame de Montespan, who was romping in his room. 'May it please God,' replied the child, ' that some day I may make as much noise as you have done.'

Duc du Maine, 1679-1736.

The Great Condé, the head of a junior branch of the House of Bourbon, was as famous for the many battles he won as for the hospitality he dispensed at his Château of Chantilly, which he had inherited from the Montmorency family. His repute as a general was sullied, however, by a contempt for human life which almost amounted to wanton cruelty, while he offended his friends by his pride and bad temper. Indeed, his character was fairly summed up by the Duchesse de Nemours when she said that he ' was a greater adept at winning battles than hearts.' In 1644 he gained the battle of Fribourg, after a hard fight, which lasted three days. The French losses were enormous, and on hearing one of his generals deplore them, Condé only replied with a laugh, ' Why, Paris daily gives to France as

many men as we have lost during all these
encounters.'   At Chantilly, when discussing a
new play with Boileau, he took up a perverse line
of argument, and became so excited that the
poet in his alarm said, ' I shall always be of the
same opinion as the Prince, especially when he
is wrong.'

' The oldest courtier,' says the Duc de Lévis
in his Memoirs, ' remembers one joke made by
Louis XIV., but they are unable to quote any
other.'   The joke in question is not of a very
high order, but it may be repeated as his solitary
achievement of the kind.   Louis had added a
menagerie to the park at Versailles, where a rare
species of turkey was bred.   He often visited
the place, and one day, being dissatisfied with
the condition of the birds, he sent for the
Inspector, who had the rank of Captain,
looked severely at him, and said, ' Captain,
if your turkeys do not thrive better I shall
cashier you, and place you at the tail of your
company.'

It is related that, when a young man, he
appeared at the meeting of the Parlement
at Vincennes in hunting dress, booted and
spurred, and with a whip in his hand.   The
President, having harangued him on the interests of the State, he is reported to have
replied, ' L'état, c'est moi ! '   As a matter
of fact he was not yet the State, for it was
still ruled by Mazarin, and it is most unlikely

that the young King should have presumed
to assert his authority so prematurely, and in a
manner at once offensive and impolitic. But it
is true that after the death of Cardinal Mazarin,
when the Portuguese Minister at the close of
an audience told the King, whose autocratic
nature had not yet been revealed, ' Oh, I shall
settle the affair with your Majesty's Ministers,'
he did reply, ' I have no Ministers ; I only
have men of business '; and about the same
time, when the Archbishop of Rouen asked
him, ' Your Majesty used to say that I should
go to the Cardinal on all matters of business—
to whom shall I apply now ? ' he answered, ' To
me.' Many famous sayings now attributed to
him were probably composed by contemporary
flatterers or posthumous admirers. For instance, he is said to have replied to the poet
Boileau, when the latter presented him with
a copy of his poem ' The Crossing of the
Rhine,' ' I should praise you more, had you
praised me less.'[1] An exaggerated laudation
of his valour could hardly have provoked this
remark from a king who revelled in the most
abject adulation, and whose frailty the most
austere prelates condoned. In fact, he handsomely rewarded Boileau for the poem. Still
less likely is it that Boileau would have ventured

*Boileau,
1636-1711.*

[1] Marguerite de Valois, the first wife of Henri
IV., used the same words to Brantôme on a similar
occasion.

to say, when the King submitted to him some verses of his own composition, 'There is nothing impossible to your Majesty. Your Majesty wished to make some bad verses, and you have succeeded.' The story is equally incredible that the King, anxious to teach a lesson to his menials and courtiers, who had treated Molière with scant ceremony, not only invited him to his own private supper-table after the performance of one of his plays, but waited on him with his own hands. We are probably indebted for this anecdote to the gossip-mongers of the day, who were anxious to enhance the personal merits of the poet-actor and to extol the enlightened patronage of the King, while, at the same time, having a fling at the members of the Court.

The most famous of the King's phrases is the one that rests on the least authority. In 1700 the Duke of Anjou left Versailles to take over the throne of Spain, and Louis, desirous of impressing the world with the security of the alliance between that country and his own, is declared to have said to him at parting, 'Il n'y a plus de Pyrenées.' The only contemporary report of the phrase is to be found in Voltaire's 'Siècle de Louis XIV.,' a notoriously untrustworthy record. Had these words been spoken, the Marquis de Dangeau would have mentioned them in his diary, in which he kept a record of the most trivial actions and utterances of the King. Dangeau, on the contrary, declares that on the occasion of the Duke of Anjou's departure it was the Spanish Ambassador who said, 'His journey will be an easy one, as the Pyrenees have now melted.' Voltaire may have manufactured the phrase, or borrowed it perchance from some adroit courtier who had improved on the Ambassador's words, and credited them to the King in their now accepted form.

But the two following incidents are fully authenticated. In 1689 Maréchal d'Uxelles, Governor of Mayence, was compelled to capitulate after a long siege, and when, later on, he appeared at Court, fearing to be reproved, he threw himself at the King's feet. But the King ordered him to rise, saying, 'Marquis, you showed your courage in the defence, and your wisdom in the capitulation.' Again, when the veteran Maréchal de Villeroy brought to Louis the news of his defeat by the Duke of Marlborough at Ramillies, the King only said, 'At our age, Maréchal, fortune no longer favours us'—words which almost redeem his lifelong heartlessness. But for the battle of Denain (1712), when Villars beat the allied forces, France might have succumbed, and the proud old King, as he threatened, would have marched at the head of his troops and perished on the field rather than submit to the degradation of an invasion and the ruin of his country.

Though he was the most callous and indifferent of husbands, he lamented the loss of the Queen, Marie Thérèse, in the words, 'God has deprived me of a consort who never gave me any cause for grief except by her death.' All that can be said of this lady, the daughter of Philippe IV. of Spain, is that she was very pious and beautiful. She spent the whole of her married life absorbed in devotional practices, or at the feet of her confessor bewailing the neglect of her royal spouse. She took no part in any of the pageantries of the Court, and no interest in any of the social, political, or literary movements of the time. Her character was of the very simplest, as may be judged from the reply she once gave to a Carmelite nun who was preparing her for some special confession she was about to make. The nun asked her whether in her youth she had ever coquetted with any young men at her father's Court at Madrid. 'Oh no, dear mother,' she replied with unaffected surprise ; 'why, there were no kings there but my father!'

The elaborate code of Court etiquette, rigorously enforced, which Louis XV. made still more stringent, and which proved so wearisome to Marie Antoinette, was drawn up by Louis XIV. Before his reign there were no prescribed rules for admission to and precedence at Court, and no

Marie Thérèse, 1638-1683.

definition of the duties of the countless officers who hedged round the person of the sovereign. No one observed these rules more strictly than the King himself. It happened that he left the palace one day with Lord Stair, the British Ambassador, and as their chariot drew up, the King motioned Lord Stair to enter it first. The Ambassador did so—to the amazement of the Court, by whom it was considered to be a breach of etiquette and a lack of deference on the Ambassador's part to have taken precedence of his Majesty. When the King heard of these remarks he said, 'On the contrary, the Ambassador was right. It would have been rude of him to have disobeyed my request.' But when, a few years before his death, the English Ambassador complained to Louis in rather freer language than he was accustomed to hear, about some works that he had ordered to be erected at Mardick in Holland, the King interrupted him with the remark, 'M. l'Ambassadeur, I have always been master in my own house, and sometimes in that of others. Do not remind me of it.'

Strong as were his passions, Louis XIV. never allowed them to betray him into an impolitic step. He set, it is true, an ominous precedent in installing his mistresses at Court, and, though there is no direct evidence on the point, he may have been influenced by Madame de Maintenon, to whom he was secretly married, in persecuting his Protestant subjects; but he never imperilled the security of the throne for the sake of his own gratification. Once he nearly committed a fatal mistake, but he drew back in time, and gave up his first, and, perhaps, his only genuine passion, in deference to dynastic and patriotic considerations.

When Mazarin was at the zenith of his power he summoned his sister, Hieronyma Mancini, and her numerous family from Italy. Honours and riches were lavished on them. The son was created a duke, the daughters, as they grew up, were married to the highest in the land. Louis XIV. was brought up in their midst, and formed an attachment for Olympe Mancini, who afterwards became the wife of the Comte de Soissons, of the House of Savoy. When Olympe's sister, Marie, appeared at Court she was eighteen and Louis was twenty. She was a bright, sparkling, and intelligent girl, but not otherwise attractive, and at first Louis left her unnoticed. Madame de Motteville, the faithful attendant of Anne of Austria, describes Marie in her Memoirs as having long thin arms, a long neck devoid of all grace, a large mouth, but good teeth; summing up her appearance with the remark that she was altogether plain. But Marie gradually developed into a beautiful woman, and her dark luminous eyes were especially praised for their latent glow of fire and genius. She was not only beautiful, she was extremely ambitious, and she set her ambition on taking the King away from her sister, and getting him into her own net, a scheme in which she succeeded. Louis fell in love with Marie, and abandoned the Comtesse de Soissons, and at one time would unquestionably have married her but for the loyalty of Mazarin. ' I should put myself with my second son at the head of the whole kingdom,' exclaimed the Queen - Mother, ' were Louis base enough to commit this act.' But there was no need for this explosion on the part of the Queen - Mother. From the very outset of the King's relations with Marie, the Cardinal was bent on foiling the designs of his niece. He placed the King's future above both his own and her prospects of enhanced greatness, and entered upon negotiations with Spain which secured advantageous terms of peace for France and a royal bride for his master. Marie, though removed from the Court, hoped against hope until the bitter end as the King still secretly corresponded with her. While making a royal progress to Bayonne to receive his future wife, the Infanta Maria Theresa, Louis met Marie Mancini for the last time, and bade her a tearful farewell. ' You are King, you weep, I leave ! ' she cried out—words which Racine almost literally repeated in his tragedy of ' Berenice.' When

Berenice was commanded to leave Rome she told Titus, 'You are Emperor, sir, and you weep.' The whole career of Marie Mancini was a romance. Mazarin married her off at once to Prince Colonna, and she was quickly and totally forgotten by Louis, who was soon engrossed by other fancies and cares. Marriage brought her no happiness; she hated her husband, and left him surreptitiously in Rome. Returning to France after a long series of adventures, Louis refused to see her, and to the end of his days he never relented. His pride had been stung by her marriage. A woman who had been loved by him should never belong to any other man. She left for Spain, where she was interned in a convent; she subsequently became reconciled to her husband, but was almost immediately afterwards divorced. She took the veil, but broke away from her conventual seclusion, returned once more to France, and died there in neglect and obscurity in 1714 —a year before the King.

Of the many fair women who in turn swayed *Louise de la* the heart of the King, Louise de la Vallière *Baume le* alone was devoid of personal ambition, and in *Blanc,* her relations with him only followed the impulse *Duchesse de* *la Vallière,* of a genuine inclination. In 1661, a year after *1642-1710.* his marriage, Louis XIV. first noticed the young girl, who, then a lady-in-waiting to the Duchesse d'Orleans (Henrietta of England), had already been fascinated by the brilliant

Louise Françoise de la Baume le Blanc.
Duchesse de la Vallière.

young sovereign. All contemporary writers
agree in extolling the grace, the loveliness, the
charm of Louise de la Vallière. For seven or
eight years she retained the King's affection, and
despite all the honours he bestowed on her, and
the semi-regal position she occupied, she never
presumed on her favour, but from first to last
she was the prey of a stricken conscience. True
to Louis for three cruel years after he had ceased
to care for her, she still remained at Court, and
bore the most humiliating insults from the man
she loved and from his new favourite Madame
de Montespan. But at last her endurance
broke down, she sought an interview with the
Queen, begged forgiveness for the offence she
had committed in loving the King and accepting
his love, and then withdrew into a Carmelite
convent in Paris, where she took the veil, and
for thirty-six years led a life of the most rigorous
penance. Two of her daughters had died in
infancy, but her son, the Comte de Vermandois,
lived till 1703. When informed of his death
she wept, but then said, 'I have shed tears
enough over the death of a son for whose birth
I have not yet sufficiently wept.' Of the other
children she had borne the King, Mademoiselle de
Blois may be mentioned, because by her marriage
with the future Regent she became the ancestress
of the present Duc d'Orleans. When Louis
XIV. heard of the death of Louise de la
Vallière he merely said, 'She has been dead

too long for me to weep for her now.' She had, in fact, ceased to exist for him the day she entered the convent, just as Marie Mancini had done on the day she became Princess Colonna.

Duquesne and Duguay-Trouin were the most illustrious of the sailors who earned a title to the favour of their sovereign. Duquesne routed the Dutch under Ruyter at Messina, beat the Mediterranean corsairs, bombarded Algiers and Genoa, but despite all these services, owing to the fact of his being a Protestant, he received no promotion. When Louis XIV. expressed to Duquesne a regret that he was precluded by his creed from adequately rewarding him, the old mariner replied, 'Yes, sire, it is true that I am a Protestant, but I thought that my services were Catholic.' 'I have given to Cæsar what belongs to Cæsar,' Duquesne proudly said to his friends ; 'it is high time I should give to God what belongs to God.' Eventually, however, the King rewarded him with a marquisate. After Duquesne's bombardment of Genoa the Doge of the Republic, who had been accused of conspiring with the corsairs, was brought to Versailles to apologise for his conduct. While he was being shown over the palace he was asked what struck him most of all it contained, and he replied, 'To see myself here.'

Duguay - Trouin was often requested by

Duquesne,
1610-1688.

Duguay-
Trouin,
1673-1736.

Louis XIV. to recount his achievements, which he did very brightly and without affectation. He was describing a fight in which one of his ships called ' La Gloire ' had been engaged, and said in the course of his story, ' I ordered " La Gloire " to follow me.' 'She has been faithful to you,' gracefully replied the King.

Unlike Duquesne, Turenne became converted to Catholicism in order to retain the King's favour. At one of the numerous sieges he was conducting he noticed that many of his officers bent down so that the cannon balls passed over their heads, but then quickly drew themselves up as if afraid of a rebuke. ' Boys! ' he exclaimed, ' you are right ; such visitors well deserve a curtsey.' His own recklessness in the field, however, brought about his untimely end. The same shot that killed him at Salzbach carried off the arm of M. de St. Hilaire, an artillery officer. M. de St. Hilaire's son ran to his father, raised him from the ground, and burst into tears. ' You should not weep for me,' said the wounded officer, ' but for the death of this great man. You may love your father, but neither you nor the country will ever find such a general again. Now go and do your duty ; I shall fare as it pleases God.' Turenne's unfailing good temper — a quality for which he has been compared to Marlborough —was exemplified in many incidents. On a hot summer's day he left his room clad in a white

Marshal Turenne, 1611-1675.

F

jacket and cap, and a servant who met him in a dark passage, mistaking him for the cook, slapped him on the back. Turenne turned round, and the man, on recognising his master, fell on his knees and cried out, ' Monseigneur, I thought you were George!' 'Even had I been George, you need not have hit so hard,' rejoined Turenne good-humouredly.

François Henri de Mont- morency, Duc de Mont- morency- Luxem- bourg, 1628-1695.

The Duc de Luxembourg became a Marshal of France after the death of Turenne. He was one of the most successful generals of the century, and was nicknamed the 'Tapissier de Notre Dame,' because of the many trophies with which he decorated the Cathedral. His great achievements on the Rhine and in Flanders in '65 and '67 provoked the jealousy of Louvois, the Minister of War. He not only accused him of being the accomplice of a gang of poisoners whose victims were some of the most illustrious persons of the day, but with carrying on an intercourse with the devil. Luxembourg was imprisoned in a foul dungeon for several weeks, and then subjected to a trial which having lasted a year, ended without a verdict, and at the end of it all he was banished from Paris for four years. He was left without a command for nine years, until 1689, when he was sent against William of Orange, whom he invariably defeated. Luxembourg was deformed. 'Shall I never beat this cursed hunchback?' exclaimed William. The words were repeated to the

Marshal, who remarked, ' Hunchback, says he?
What does he know of it? He never saw my
back!'

Colbert, the ablest Minister of Louis XIV.,
was universally unpopular owing to his financial
and fiscal reforms, and the heavy taxes he was
obliged to impose on the people to meet the
cost of numerous wars. He fought bravely
to the last, though his ungrateful sovereign
sacrificed him to Louvois. When Colbert was
on his deathbed, the King, who was ailing at
the time, and perhaps stung by remorse, sent
him a letter begging him to take care of himself, and expressing the hope that he would soon
recover. But Colbert, without opening the mis-
sive, replied to the messenger, 'I will hear no
more of the King. Let me die in peace. It is
to the King of kings I now have to answer.
Had I done for God what I have done for that
man, I should have found salvation ten times
over, and now I do not know what will become of me.'

Colbert,
1619-1683.

Louis XIV. maintained a dignified pose
until the last hour of his life. On his deathbed he said to Madame de Maintenon, 'I
was always told that it was very hard to make
up one's mind to die, but I do not find it
so difficult.' 'Oh, sire!' she answered, 'it is
only difficult for those who have some affection
in their hearts, or some hate, or any restitution
to make.' 'As far as making restitution,'

replied the King, 'I owe none as a private individual, and as for what I owe the kingdom, I hope for the mercy of God.'   Then he turned to a page who was kneeling weeping by the bedside and said to him, 'Why do you weep? Did you believe me to be immortal?'

Louis XV.

THE REIGN OF LOUIS XV.

THOUGH the English people, like the French, suffered misgovernment and oppression at the hands of some of their sovereigns, they obtained comparative freedom at an early period of their history. In England the nobles and the people, on the whole, made common cause in the struggle for liberty, and the attainment of national prosperity and imperial greatness was due to their own initiative. In France the case was different. There, for many centuries, the King, the nobility, and the people were separated by a wide chasm. As the King was an autocrat, the fortunes of the State rose or decayed mainly according to his ability or incapacity to rule wisely. But the feudal system made the King dependent on the nobles, and the chief object of his policy was to shake off their yoke. The nobles, a numerous and powerful class, on their side derived their privileges from the Crown, and they were incessantly endeavouring to encroach on its prerogatives to enhance their own influence. The people were no better than serfs ; overtaxed by the King and ill-treated by the nobles. Conflicts constantly arose between the three orders. At times the King combined with the people against the pretensions of the nobles ; at others the nobles combined with the people against the despotism of the King. On the whole, however, the nobles were loyal to the throne, and to their motto, ' God and the King.' But they belonged to a turbulent and warlike race who loved fighting for its own sake, and cared little with whom they fought as long as they fought with some one, whether the infidel, the foreigner, the King, the people, or each other. In the end the King had always triumphed, because his authority and his resources were greater than those of his opponents, and because the patriotic sentiment of the country was more closely identified with his cause. In the last resort, the sanction of the King was the only security the nobles had for the preservation of their privileges, and the people could not effectively combine against the throne because of their oppressed condition, their poverty, and their dispersal over a great area of country at a time when no communications, worthy of the name, existed. So they bore their yoke silently and sullenly.

The seventeenth century witnessed a great change. When Louis XIV. died the power of the nobles had vanished, the people had become homogeneous, civilisation had progressed, trade

had expanded, a great middle class—as wealthy
and intelligent as the British—was cementing
together the various sections of the population.
The Crown alone remained what it had been.
The King was still an autocrat. At the accession of Louis XV. to the throne, the fate of
France hung in the balance. Strict economy
would have repaired the economic condition of·
the country, a firm hand would have crushed
the extravagant pretensions of the nobility, and
equitable concessions would have satisfied the
people. By a sound administration the army
and the navy would have been placed in an
efficient state, a strong policy would have maintained order at home and peace abroad ; and last,
but not least, a good example set in his private
character by the first personage in the land would
have checked, if it did not cure, the growing
dissoluteness of the upper classes; in fine, the
Revolution would not have become inevitable.

As it happened, Louis XV. was perhaps one *Louis XV.,*
of the worst rulers and worst men mentioned *1710-1774.*
in history. Most, if not all, the bad men
we read of had some redeeming feature. Sarda-
napalus knew how to die, Nero was fond of
poetry and art, Charles IX. saved his Protestant nurse from the Massacre of St. Bartholomew, James II. preferred his faith to
his crown ; even the crimes of an ordinary
highwayman, a Cartouche or a Macheath,
were palliated by occasional good-nature or

picturesque adventure. Louis XV. lived like a satrap and died like a coward. When Damiens grazed his skin with a penknife he went into hysterics, and ordered the half-crazy wretch to be put to death by the slowest and most exquisite tortures his physicians could contrive. He despised men of letters ; he turned his back on Voltaire when he appeared at Court ; he had no appreciation for the grand conceptions of art. The magnificent staircase of Versailles—a triumph of architecture—he pulled down, and he converted a stately chamber into small apartments for his private convenience.

He never sought an opportunity to prove his bravery. His piety was the grossest superstition, and he allowed his subjects to be persecuted for their beliefs or their opinions. He showed no concern for the welfare of his people ; they were simply a brute mass to be taxed to supply him with money. He never took any interest in the affairs of the State ; they bored him, as everything bored him with the exception of hunting and gambling and women ; and even his relations with women were unrelieved by the slightest touch of romance. Affairs of State he left to Ministers whose appointment was the work of his mistresses, though his cunning found a congenial outlet in tortuous intrigues behind their backs. He was not deficient in natural ability and wit, but he was too weak and suspicious, too selfish, indolent, and shy to do himself justice. His one desire from his earliest youth was to be taken out of himself, to be relieved of his incurable *ennui*. The pursuit of the meanest objects, such as cooking, embroidery, and gossiping, engrossed him more than a meeting of his Council. He was incapable of any great effort, or of genuine affection for either man or woman. He was unpatriotic and depraved, an infamous ruler and a despicable man.

Yet there is a fascination about the French eighteenth century, the period between 1715 and 1789, which will always endure. It was an age unique in its idiosyncrasies, and was totally dissimilar from any that preceded or followed it. It seems to have suddenly sprung into life, and to have as suddenly expired. Its men and its women appeared to derive none of their distinctive characteristics from their ancestors, nor did they transmit them to their descendants. More remarkable still, many of those who survived to a later period only preserved its special characteristics during its span ; thenceforward its authors wrote in a different style ; its artists lost their art—for everything appertaining to that period was carried to its extreme, its degradation as well as its eminence. France never sank so low as during the reign of Louis XV. Except for Port Mahon and Fontenoy (and Fontenoy was won by a German commander by the aid of Irish troops) her

armies and her fleets were invariably beaten.
Her statesmen — Choiseul perhaps excepted —
were incompetent, and brought moral corruption
to the worst pitch.   France was financially
bankrupt, and in the polity of nations she ceased
to be of any account.

But from the decay of the French eighteenth
century rose the perfume that surrounded
it with so much glamour and glory.   The
upper classes were forced by the very excess
of their depravity to veil it in a disguise
of the most seductive refinement.   Reckless
extravagance led to an exceptional splendour of
architecture, decoration, furniture, uniforms,
equipages, and dress.   The upper classes, un-
concerned for the graver interests of life,
threw all their energies into its frivolities,
investing them with a charm which has never
been equalled.   And to a great extent these
energies found ample scope in the field of
letters.   The prostration produced by the events
of the latter years of the reign of Louis XIV.
had its inevitable result in the wretched emascu-
lation of the aristocracy, which marked the
eighteenth century.   But a buoyant and capable
nation like the French will, under all circumstances, find an outlet for their genius and
national impulses, and as the then prevailing
conditions precluded them from excelling in
other spheres, they broke out into literature.
Almost every educated man and woman be-

came a writer, and a writer of note. The mere
bulk of the books they have left would be
surprising for its magnitude, were it not more
for their almost uniform excellence in point of
style. And in a yet higher sphere the eighteenth
century claims imperishable renown. But for
its vices, its great school of philosophers might
not have sprung into existence. To expose
these vices was their mission, and they kindled a
flame that soon illumined the country, being the
first to teach those principles to which in a great
degree France owes her liberty.

The most trivial events and details of the
King's life have been recorded for our edifica-
tion, but he seems to have said few noteworthy
things. As has been said, he was no fool, and
was able to gauge accurately enough the true
worth of his associates, though so long as they
amused him he was content. The Comte de
St. Germain observed to him one day, that 'to
appreciate mankind one must be a confessor, a
Minister, or the head of the police '—' Or the
King,' added Louis XV. While at supper
with the King, M. de Chauvelin, one of his
Ministers, suddenly dropped dead. Shortly
afterwards the King went out for a drive, and one
of the team fell, and died on the spot. 'Why,
this is just like poor Chauvelin !' was the King's
only funeral oration on his departed Minister.
There is only one reply of Louis XV.'s which
can be quoted as reflecting any credit upon

him.   When on a visit to the printing press
of the Ministry of War he was given a paper
and a pair of glasses to read it by.   The paper
contained a high-flown panegyric of himself,
but he put it down with the remark, 'These
glasses are too strong ; they magnify too
much.'

It is not intended to write an essay on the
social condition of France in the eighteenth
century, or to analyse its peculiar standard of
morality ; but so much may be said : that the
deplorable example set by the Regent, the Duc
d'Orleans, and by his successor at the head of
the Government, the Duc de Bourbon, and, in
a still more barefaced and degrading way, by
Louis XV. himself, was only too eagerly imi-
tated by the prominent personages of the land.
At the same time it is a curious fact that while
the most licentious depravity became the accepted
fashion, and it was almost a point of honour for
those personages to display their contempt for
the marriage tie, and for both sexes to vie with
each other in parading their vices, yet at no time
in history was more deferential homage out-
wardly paid to woman, or a more minute regard for appearances displayed in matters of tone
and demeanour.   Never did woman stand on a
higher pinnacle of supremacy than at that period,
and whether for good or evil, in all relations
of life her power became paramount.   Women
ruled at Versailles, in the salons of Paris they

Madame de Pompadour.

brought politicians, artists, and men of letters into notoriety. By their influential connections they became the chief source of patronage and preferment, and by their personal graces and cultivated intelligence they stamped their individuality on the whole tendency of the age. No wonder, therefore, that in looking at this epoch, the first name that forces itself on one's notice is not that of a church dignitary, a soldier, a statesman, or a man of letters, but of the foremost woman of the day, Madame de Pompadour. A fortune-teller had predicted in her youth that she would become the mistress of the King. She never forgot the prediction, and made it her whole aim to fulfil it. Nor was she ungrateful to the fortunate seer, for after her death a paper was found among her effects, showing that she had allowed that individual a pension of six hundred francs.

Jeanne Antoinette Poisson, Marquise de Pompadour, 1721-1764.

Madame de Pompadour was the daughter of a fraudulent army-contractor, and was married to the nephew of a Fermier-General. From the moment she first attracted the King's notice when hunting in the forest of Senart (where she went driving with that express object on alternate days in a blue phæton, dressed in pink satin, and in a pink phæton, dressed in blue), this very remarkable woman to the hour of her death never lost her hold on Louis XV. Once only she was on the brink of disgrace. Louis XV. had been wounded in 1757 by Damiens. The injury was slight, but the King's terror was intense, and he was urged to make peace with his God by dismissing, his all-powerful mistress. Madame de Pompadour would have obeyed the command to quit Versailles had not her staunch friend, the Duchesse de Mirepoix, warned her that she 'who quits the game loses it.' The King soon recovered, and the Marquise remained. To retain her hold over the King she encouraged his vices, drove him into deeper abysses of immorality, and irretrievably lowered the dignity of the throne. Her influence in politics was disastrous, for she was led altogether by fancy and vanity. The adroit flatteries and magnificent gifts which the Empress Maria Theresa condescended to bestow on her, resulted in involving France in the Seven Years' War. She promoted her creatures to responsible positions, and ejected competent men from their offices if they ran counter to her whims. The Prince de Soubise, the most incapable officer in the army, was by her desire made a marshal, and was sent to oppose Frederick the Great. After his defeat at Rossbach his incapacity supplied the lampoonists with their chief stock-in-trade. M. de Maurepas, a distinguished Minister, was banished from Paris for twenty-five years for having amused a supper-party with a couplet in which he made sport of her charms. Her personal extravagance was on a gigantic scale. Despite the impoverished condition of the treasury and the prevailing distress she purchased or built thirty-six country or town residences— the best-known of which are Bellevue and the Elysée,—and in many of them she never set foot. She formed a precious library and a collection of works of art, which it took her brother upwards of a year to dispose of by auction after her death.

But though merciless in avenging anything in the shape of a personal insult, she was of a kindly disposition, showed much tact both in her relations with the royal family and with the most exalted members of the aristocracy, many of whom paid her fulsome attention. She was assiduously courted by men of letters, on whose works and opinions she set a high value. It happened one evening at supper that the King was discussing the day's sport with his companions, and the Duc de Nivernois suddenly remarked, 'It is strange that we should find so much pleasure in shooting partridges in the park at Versailles, and in killing others or occasionally being killed ourselves on the frontier, without knowing precisely what it is that does kill.' 'Alas!' replied Madame de Pompadour, 'it is the same with most things. I do not know what rouge is composed of, and you would embarrass me considerably were you to ask me how my silk stockings were made.' 'It is a pity,' said the Duc de la Vallière, turning to the King, 'that your Majesty has confiscated the "Encyclopædia"; it would give us the answers to our questions.' A volume of the work was sent for, and Madame de Pompadour discovered the difference between the old Spanish rouge used by the ladies of Madrid and that used by the ladies of Paris; while she was still further gratified on learning how her silk stockings were made. 'Oh, excellent book!' she exclaimed. 'Sire, you have confiscated this storehouse of useful things in order to be its sole possessor and the only scholar in the kingdom.' From that day forward she advised the chief contributor to the 'Encyclopædia' to be careful, so as not to provoke the hostility of the King, and she obtained a pension for D'Alembert, one of its founders. Voltaire, the mouthpiece, so to speak, of public opinion, unceasingly sang her praises. But she tempted Rousseau in vain with the offer of a grant. A passage in his 'Emile,' stating that 'the wife of a coalheaver is more estimable than the mistress of a king,' excited her anger, but the only concession she could obtain from the philosopher was the substitution of 'prince' for 'king.' She was accomplished in the highest degree, had exquisite taste, was a perfect comedian and singer, a munificent patron of art, and no mean artist herself, and not only established the porcelain manufactory of Sèvres, but contributed greatly to the embellishment and improvement of Paris. Boucher painted many portraits of her, and as these pictures, both great and small, still exist, it is easy to become familiar with her appearance. Her features were not of a classical type, but she had a beautiful figure, and possessed all the grace and charm of the Parisienne — that peculiar power of adapting herself to all circumstances and conditions which, among women, the French at all times and in all classes have most eminently possessed. She was sitting for her portrait [1] to Latour, the famous pastel painter, when the King entered the room bringing the news of the defeat of the French army at Rossbach. ' Why are you distressed?' she asked; 'after us the deluge!' Seven years later, as she lay dying, and the priest having administered the sacrament to her, was bidding her farewell, she said with a smile, ' Wait a moment, M. le Curé, and we shall go out together.'

Louis XV. bore the yoke of Madame de Pompadour so long not because he was still attached to her, but because she always succeeded in amusing or providing him with amusement, though the effort cost her her life. Her friend, Madame d'Esparbés, a young, flighty, and beautiful woman, had for a while fascinated the monarch. One day he reproved her for the number of her intrigues. ' Yes,' he went on saying, ' most of my subjects may boast that they have found favour in your eyes.'

' Oh, sire! '

' Take, for instance, the Duc de Choiseul? '

---

[1] This portrait is now in the museum at St. Quentin.

' He is such a powerful Minister ! '

' But the Maréchal de Richelieu ? '

' He is so witty ! '

' But De Monville ? ' (Master of the Woods and Forests of Normandy).

' He has such a good figure ! '

' How about the Duc d'Aumont — he has none of these qualities ? '

' Oh, sire, he is so devoted to your Majesty ! '

Before the advent of Madame de Pompadour, the daughters of the Marquis de Nesles had for a time captivated the vagrant fancy of the King. *Comtesse de Mailly, 1710-1751.* The eldest, the Comtesse de Mailly, was said to have been brought to the notice of Louis XV. by Cardinal Fleury, who, anxious to retain the entire control of affairs, feared no interference from the new favourite. It is certain that he connived at Madame de Mailly's position at Court, while her husband was silenced by a gift of money and installed at Versailles, and her father was banished for venturing to object to the arrangement. Thus such affairs were managed in those times. For eight years Madame de Mailly enjoyed the questionable happiness of the King's affection, but in 1742 she had to retire from Court. At first she intrigued to be recalled, but ultimately she desisted from the attempt, and devoted the rest of her life to penance and pious discipline. One day as she was entering a church where a famous preacher was drawing large crowds, a man who saw the people making way for her exclaimed, ' What a fuss about such a person ! ' ' Well, as you know her, pray for her,' mildly replied the fallen favourite.

The disgrace of Madame de Mailly had been effected by her sister, the Marquise de Tournelles, whom Louis XV. afterwards created Duchesse de Chateauroux. She was said to be *Duchesse de* ' as high as the mountains,' because of her haughty *Chateau-* *roux,* bearing, but whatever her faults, she was intelli- *1717-1744.* gent, ambitious, and above the usual pettiness of her kind. She readily listened to the advice of her friends who deplored that their sovereign was indifferent to the grave national issues that were at stake. They lamented that his Ministers should be allowed ' to play pitch-and-toss ' with the government of the realm, display- ing no concern at the disastrous news that was coming in from abroad. Impatient of great achievements and weary of the paltry super- ficiality of her life at Court, Madame de Chateauroux's pride was hurt by the undignified conduct of the King, so she undertook to rouse him from his apathy and sloth, and urged him to place himself at the head of his army in the field. She incessantly harassed the King, until at last he cried out, ' You are killing me ! ' ' So much the better, sire,' she replied, ' for the King must be brought back to life again.' And she succeeded in her object, for Louis XV. went to the seat of war. Had Madame de

Chateauroux then left the scene, her name might have come down to us with some honour, but she accompanied the King to the frontier, and the gravest scandals ensued. The sequel to the story was dramatic. The King suddenly fell ill, and the Duchess was ignominiously driven from the camp. When Louis recovered he summoned her back to Versailles, but on the way she was attacked with a serious illness, and she soon afterwards died in the arms of the sister whom she had supplanted, but who had forgotten and forgiven the injury. The news of Madame de Chateauroux's death overwhelmed the King with grief, and even affected the Queen, who spent the evening alone in her room instead of joining the company at the Duchesse de Luynes', as she had arranged. In the night she jumped up in a state of great excitement and called for her waiting-woman. 'Gracious heavens!' she cried out, 'I thought I saw the poor duchess. Suppose she were to return.' 'Were she to do so,' was the reply, 'your Majesty would not have the first visit.'

Jean Vaubernier, Comtesse du Barry, 1743-1793.

Five years after Madame de Pompadour's death, the Comtesse du Barry took up her abode at Versailles. It would have been better for France, as for herself, had she never been lifted out of obscurity. She encouraged the extravagance of the King, and was the cause of the dismissal of the Duc de Choiseul. But

La Comtesse du Barri.

Marie Leczinska

she knew no better, nor could she be expected to do so. The blame lay with the King, who was now dead to every sense of honour and duty. Though flighty, frivolous, and incapable of any lofty conception, Madame du Barry was not bad by nature. When the Revolution broke out she ran the greatest risks, and even courted death, to assist her friends who were in trouble. She offered her fortune, in the humblest terms, to assist Marie Antoinette, and gave jewels as well as large sums of money to relieve the necessities of imprisoned or fugitive royalties. Her generosity and her devotion to a lost cause marked her out for the cupidity and vengeance of the Revolutionary party ; she was dragged before the Tribunal and sentenced to death. But almost alone among its victims, she faltered and cried on the way to the guillotine, and her last pleading words to the executioner were, 'Mercy, sir! Mercy! but one moment more!'[1]

Speaking of Madame du Barry to the Duc de Noailles, Louis XV. once said half apologetically, 'I am aware that I have succeeded Monsieur de Sainte Foix.' 'Yes, sire,' replied the Duc, 'just as your Majesty has succeeded King Pharamond.' *Duc de Noailles, 1713-1793.*

It is some satisfaction to turn to the Queen, Marie Leczinska, whom history has painfully neglected in favour of the ladies who usurped *Marie Leczinska, 1703-1768.*

[1] 'Grâce, Monsieur le Bourreau ! un moment de plus !'

her position.   In 1704 her father, Stanislas, had
been elected King of Poland, but after a troubled
reign of seven years a hostile faction, supported
by Russia, drove him from the country.   His
friend, Charles XII. of Sweden, invested him
with a small German principality, but this too
he soon had to surrender.   He then found
an asylum at Wyssenbourg in Alsace.   Some
years later he was recalled to Poland by his
party, but he never gained ground, and was
obliged to return to his retreat at Wyssenbourg.
Finally, by the Treaty of Vienna in 1738, he
was declared sovereign of Lorraine, whose
previous ruler now became Duke of Tuscany,
and subsequently Emperor of Germany.   It
was arranged that after the death of Stanislas,
whose daughter had married Louis XV., Lorraine
was to revert to France.   When that marriage
took place there was no prospect, however, of
the magnificent dowry which Marie Leczinska
eventually brought her husband.   She was then
only the penniless daughter of a dethroned king,
without any of the personal attractions which
might have won her a crown ; and she was
twenty-two years of age—seven years older than
Louis.   She was well educated, spoke French
and German perfectly, and had many accom-
plishments.   Her complexion was brilliant and
her bearing graceful, but she was short and
decidedly plain.   Her piety and goodness of
heart were highly commended, though it may

safely be assumed that these qualities weighed little with those who chose her to be their queen. How then did this choice come to be made?

Louis was still a mere child when he was betrothed by the Regent to a Spanish Infanta. After the death of the Regent in 1723, the Duc de Bourbon governed France, but he in turn was governed by a woman, the beautiful and ambitious Marquise de Prié. The chief object of this worthy couple was to thwart the hopes of the young Duc d'Orleans, the heir-presumptive, whom they hated, and to preclude the possibility of his ever succeeding to the Crown. The marriage with the Infanta would have answered their purpose, but for reasons both political and private, it was broken off, and another bride had to be found for the King. Meanwhile the Duc de Bourbon, urged by his mother to secure a wife for himself, asked Stanislas for the hand of his daughter. But Madame de Prié was alarmed by the far too flattering account she received of Marie's appearance and intelligence, so that to obviate the risk of losing the Duc de Bourbon, she put a stop to his courtship, and to make quite sure of keeping him in her power, she settled that the Polish princess should share the throne of France. The wedding was celebrated with great pomp, and for a few months the Queen enjoyed unalloyed happiness. She was in love with Louis, and she remained true to that love during the whole of her long married life. She at first made a favourable impression on Louis, but he was not a man to care long for so refined and high-minded a woman, and being selfish and callous, he soon began to treat her with marked coldness. The first blow fell when the Duc de Bourbon, for whom, as she owed to him her great position, she had an affectionate regard, was disgraced and banished, and his office bestowed on Cardinal Fleury. Fleury, fearing her influence on the King, as Madame de Prie had feared her influence on the Duc de Bourbon, intrigued against her with most malign hostility, and had little difficulty in completely estranging the King from her. Yet she endured the King's studied indifference without complaint, and even to his Minister she bore no ill-will. 'I am overburdened with work,' he told her one day ; 'I shall lose my head !' 'Mind you do not,' replied Marie, 'I very much doubt that whoever found it would care to give up such a good article.' The parsimonious Minister, to effect a penny-wise economy, had removed and turfed over a magnificent waterfall at Marly, so that when he observed of the Treaty of Vienna, 'Believe, madame, that the Duchy of Lorraine will be far better for your father than the kingdom of Poland'—'Yes,' she archly replied, 'for much the same reason that a lawn is preferable to a cascade.' When she was advised to counteract Fleury's animosity by giving her support to another Minister who was politically opposed to him, she said, 'I should like to see justice done, but I fear vengeance too much.'

Louis treated the Queen with increasing coldness, and gradually gave way more and more to those passions which turned her very existence into a martyrdom. Yet she suffered in silence, for she loved the man who daily insulted her in her devotion as a wife and her pride as a queen. The Comtesse de Mailly and the Duchesse de Chateauroux were made members of her household, their presence being thus forced on her. Then in 1744 the Duchess accompanied the King to the wars, whilst the Queen was ordered to remain at Versailles. The sisters never spared the Queen any humiliation, though, in contrast with them, Madame de Pompadour from first to last treated her with the greatest deference. 'As there must be a mistress at Versailles, better she than another,' exclaimed the poor Queen, whose meek disposition was never more signally displayed than on the occasion of Madame de Pompadour's presentation at Court. Instead of making some commonplace remark on her gown, as was customary at these presentations, Marie spoke to Madame de Pompadour of Madame de Saissac, the only great lady with whom the latter was as yet acquainted. The Marquise was so overcome by the Queen's condescension and kindness, that she confusedly replied, 'I have, madame, the greatest desire to please you.' When the King obliged the Queen to appoint Madame de Pompadour a lady of his household, she suffered this new humiliation with the patience of a saint : 'Sire,' she said, 'I have a God in heaven who gives me strength to bear my sufferings, and I have a King on earth whom I shall always obey.'

The Queen knew how to assert herself when she thought well to do so. One of her ladies complained to her of some trivial dereliction of duty of which her Majesty's 'servants' had been apparently guilty. 'Pray know,' sternly replied Marie, 'that you have servants, but I have not. I have officers of the household who have the honour of serving me.' It was that same consciousness of what was due to her as a Queen and what was due from her as a Queen that made her excel in the performance of the daily arduous and ornate functions of Court life, so that even Louis XV. himself was unable to withhold his approval of her dignity and grace. After Madame de Pompadour's death the Queen wrote of her to President Henault, 'She is no more thought of than if she had never existed. So goes the world; is it worth loving?' Madame de Pompadour was, as a matter of fact, actually forgotten before she had ceased to live.

In the privacy of her own room and the

society of her children and friends Marie found some compensation for the bitterness of her life. The young Dauphin, to whom she was fondly attached, she often called Barnabè. ' Why do you give me this name, mother?' he once asked her. 'Because Barnabè means the child of solace.' ' And why,' he asked her another day, ' are your prayers more fervent and longer than those of the most fervent Carmelites?' 'Because my wants are greater than theirs; they are always with God; I am always with the world.' In that world she might have occupied the position for which she was eminently suited, grouping round the throne a brilliant and distinguished circle, but others took her place in the ' King's apartments ' and played her part in their own way. The Queen was content to see only a few intimate friends, in whose company the playfulness of her wit, no less than the seriousness of her mind, had full scope for development. History was one of the chief subjects of conversation at these gatherings, at which the Queen's Chief Equerry, the Comte de Tessé, was often present. The Queen liked the Count, though he was not remarkable for cleverness. The great deeds of valour which the French nobility had performed in the past were once being reviewed when the Queen, addressing him, said, ' But as for you, M. de Tessé, the whole of your family have been famous in war?' 'Oh, madame,' he enthusiastically replied, ' we have

all been killed in serving our master.' 'It is
fortunate,' replied the Queen, 'that *you* have
been left to tell us it.' When he talked of his
daughter-in-law, to whom he was devoted,
M. de Tessé always became deeply moved.
'Which of her qualities do you prize most?'
the Queen asked him one day. 'Her kindness,
madame,' he said, half choking with emotion ;
'she is as soft, as soft as—a good carriage.'
'A comparison worthy of an equerry,' the
Queen remarked.

The Dauphin died in 1765, and the Dauphine,
Marie Joséphe de Saxe, soon afterwards. Marie
Leczinska was attached to her, though she was
afflicted with a bad temper and was disliked by
her household. Even during her last illness she so
ill-used her ladies that the Duchesse de Lauragais
sarcastically said to them, 'This Princess is so
kind that she is unwilling to hurt any one even
by her death.' King Stanislas passed away soon
after, and the Queen, unable to survive their loss,
died in 1768, after a painful and lingering illness.
She bore her sufferings heroically, and often said,
'I thank God for being enabled to remember the
grand example the Dauphin has left me.' The
King during her last days paid her unusual
attention, which was more than might have
been expected from him.

Visitors to Versailles are shown the portrait of Marie Leczinska by Nattier, perhaps
the best picture in the palace. Genuine

benevolence beams from the Queen's face, which
is that of a plain, middle-aged woman with
features distinctly Slav.   But for this portrait,
every inch of which bespeaks high breeding, all
recollection of her has faded out of the palace.
The custodian points out the shrubberies where
young Louis talked love to La Vallière, the
terrace where Montespan walked surrounded by
courtiers, Madame de Maintenon's apartment,
and the stairs by which Marie Antoinette
escaped from her assassins ; but of Marie
Leczinska there is no reminiscence.[1] She was
too simple for the splendour of the palace in
which her sad life was caged, too good for the
atmosphere of intrigue with which the Court
was impregnated, too pure for the dissoluteness
of her generation.   Had she been beautiful,
writers and poets would have extolled her
charms in prose and in verse, scandal would
have been busy with her name, and she would
have become an eighteenth-century heroine ;
yet none deserves more the regard and notice
of posterity.

Considering how many biographies and
sketches of the prominent women of the
eighteenth century have been written, it may
well be a matter for surprise that the Duchesse
de Montmorency-Luxembourg should not have

Madeleine de Villeroy, Duchesse de Montmorency-Luxembourg, 1707-1787.

[1] The apartments of Madame de Pompadour and
Madame du Barry have been pulled down in the course
of alterations.

been deemed worthy of some notice. Of the many 'great ladies' of the time she was one of the most remarkable and most characteristic. She was married when almost still a child—all great ladies were then married out of the nursery — to the Marquis de Boufflers, and on his death to the Duc de Luxembourg, a Marshal of France. She was as beautiful as she was clever, and as haughty as she was frail ; but after her second marriage she reformed, became a leader of fashion, and the arbiter of good breeding and manners. Like most ladies of her order, she patronised men of letters, and was on the best of terms with Rousseau especially. The philosopher, who quarrelled with all his friends, and would accept no favours from them, deigned to avail himself of the offer of a cottage in her park, where he read to her the manuscript of his 'Nouvelle Héloise' and 'Emile'; and when the censor ordered Rousseau's arrest after the publication of the latter work, she assisted him to escape from France. Her salon was one of the most brilliant of the time, and her personal influence was so great that she was said to have the power of making or unmaking reputations. The alleged exercise of this prerogative by the Duchess provoked the cynical *Prince de* remark from the Prince de Ligne that 'those *Ligne,* who usually make or mar reputations are *1735-1814.* those who have none of their own.' She was inordinately proud of the greatness of her husband's family—perhaps with some reason, for the Duc de Montmorency was called the 'First Christian Baron.'[1] The Dauphin once tauntingly asked her whether she was acquainted with all the great deeds the Montmorencies had performed. 'Sir,' she replied, 'I know the history of France!' She was somewhat less enamoured of the prestige of her own family. Her brother, the Duc de Villeroy, lamenting to her the death of his only son, said, 'Alas! there will be no more Villeroys.' 'Well, then,' she replied, 'the world will do without them, as it did until three centuries ago.' But she was not good-natured, and she made many enemies by her caustic tongue. At an evening party some friends were discussing with her the merits of a line from a poem by Delille—

And these two great ruins were consoling each other [2]—

when the door opened and a servant announced 'Madame de la Reyniere (the wife of the famous Fermier-General) and the Bailly de Breteuil,' both middle-aged. 'Decidedly,' muttered the Duchess maliciously, 'the line is a good one.' She was worldly in the highest degree, and attached supreme importance to outward forms. Staying over a Sunday with the Prince de Conti, the party, before going to church,

[1] Premier Baron Chrétien.
[2] (Et ces deux grands débris se consolaient entre eux.)

were looking through the prayer-book, when she said that the style of the prayers showed a want of 'good breeding'; they were, in fact, rather vulgarly written. It was suggested to her that so long as the prayers were said with true devotion and piety, it did not matter whether their style was good or bad. 'No,' replied the Duchess, 'I do not believe it,' and no amount of persuasion could induce her to alter her opinion.

Marie Thérèse Rodet, Madame Geoffrin, 1699-1777.

Madame Geoffrin affords perhaps the most telling illustration of the position women were able to attain in France at that time when endowed with personal charm and intellectual gifts. Madame Geoffrin was of humble birth, being the daughter of a Groom of the Chambers in the Royal Household, and the wife of a glass manufacturer. Her husband died leaving her a large fortune, and thenceforward she devoted herself to society, and collected in her salon the most prominent artists, the most brilliant men of letters, as well as the most exclusive leaders of fashion. In her youth she had been beautiful, but, unlike most of her contemporaries, scandal had never glanced upon her name, and as soon as her looks faded, to use her own words, she 'settled down without bargaining.' Her tastes and her years 'went in harness like a pair of well-matched horses.' With infinite tact, instead of endeavouring to eclipse her company by her own talk, she excelled in making her visitors display their talents to the best advantage. ' I may compare myself to a small circular tree,' she once said to Fontenelle, ' whose branches extend on all sides—I join a little in everything, I know a little of everything.' Even the Abbé de St. Pierre, who was considered a first-class social bore, was declared to be brilliant in her salon. ' I am but an instrument,' he modestly said to his hostess, ' on which you have played with success.' Count Poniatowski, a distinguished Polish gentleman, was so delighted with Madame Geoffrin that he spoke of her as his ' wife,' and sent his five sons to Paris to be educated under her care. One of these, Stanislas Augustus, became so devoted to her that he called her ' mother,' and on being elected King of Poland invited her to Warsaw. A true Parisian, she had never left her native city, and it took her upwards of a year to prepare for the journey. At Vienna, where her fame had preceded her, she was received with semi-regal honours. Prince Kaunitz, the Prime Minister, overwhelmed her with civilities ; the Emperor Joseph II., on seeing her, stopped his chariot, went up to the door of her carriage, and expressed his delight at making her acquaintance. The Empress Maria Theresa paid her the compliment of according her an interview. ' What a charming little Archduchess,' said Madame Geoffrin, half to herself, on seeing Marie Antoinette, then a lovely child of twelve ; ' I should like to carry her off.' ' Carry her off

H

by all means,' answered the Empress, smiling. Madame Geoffrin spent five months at the court of her royal friend in Poland, but though invited to Russia by the Empress Catherine, she declined the invitation, and returned to Paris and her beloved salon.

In a letter to his friend Gray, dated 25th January 1766, Horace Walpole gives a long account of Parisian society, with 'pictures,' to use his own expression, of the leading ladies.

Marie Thérèse de Brancas, Comtesse de Rochefort, 1716-1782.

'Madame de Rochfort' (*sic*), he writes, 'is different from all the rest. Her understanding is just and delicate, with a finesse of wit that is the result of reflection. Her manner is soft and feminine, and though a *savante*, without any declared pretensions. . . .' These traits—wit, knowledge, gracefulness, and modesty—gave the Comtesse de Rochefort a unique position with the literary and scientific as well as with the fashionable women of the day. Duclos, the historian, in the course of a conversation with her and the Duchesse de Mirepoix, was contrasting honest women with those who were not honest, and said, ' As for the latter, anything you say shocks them ; they are more bashful, in fact, than the others.' Following this, he launched forth into a series of highly-flavoured stories, until he was stopped by Madame de Rochefort with the remark, ' Pray be careful, M. Duclos, do not consider us *too* honest! '

The Comte de Charolais, a prince of the

House of Condé, enjoyed the questionable dis- *Charles de* tinction of being the greatest scoundrel of his *Bourbon,* *Comte de* time. His iniquities were already common talk *Charolais,* when he filled up the measure by his well-known *1700-1761.* exploit of shooting some slaters who were working at his house, and laughing merrily as his victims rolled off the roof. This wanton act of savagery greatly incensed the King. 'I will forgive you,' Louis XV. said to the Count, who begged for mercy, 'but you must know that if you commit any fresh offence I shall pardon the person who kills you, whoever it may be.' Charolais was insolent as well as brutal. One day he met the Duc de Brissac in the house of a lady to whom he was attached, and addressing him in an offensive and menacing tone, told him to 'Get out!' ('Sortez!'). 'Your ancestors,' replied De Brissac, 'would have said, "Come out!"' ('Sortons!').

Cardinal Fleury has attained historic repute, *Cardinal* less by his merits as a statesman than owing to *Fleury,* *1653-1743.* fortuitous circumstances. Little can be said against him in his private capacity. He was distinguished for his good temper, his courtesy of manner, and uprightness of character; qualities for which he was selected to be the tutor of the King, when, at the age of five, Louis XV. succeeded to the throne. The royal pupil as he grew up became devoted to his tutor, who was one of the few individuals to whom he showed any affection. But to gain this affection Fleury had fostered the pernicious inclinations of the youth. Instead of training him seriously for the duties of his position, he preferred to ignore his misconduct, while in order to retain his untrammelled supremacy in public affairs, the Cardinal encouraged the King's apathy and dislike for work. In 1726, when Louis was sixteen years old, he appointed Fleury his chief Minister, and the Cardinal remained at his post until he died in 1743, at the age of ninety.

The contrast between Fleury and his two predecessors, Cardinal Dubois and the Duc de Bourbon, has perhaps raised him unduly in the estimation of posterity. He owes his fame to one great achievement—the negotiation of the Treaty of Vienna—under which France secured the reversion of the Duchy of Lorraine on the death of King Stanislas. But, on the other hand, to avoid going to war with England he allowed the navy and trade of France to decay, while to sap the power of Austria he entered into an alliance with Prussia through which he drifted into the Austrian War of Succession. Fleury was parsimonious, and as far as the personal acquisition of wealth was concerned, disinterested, and consequently died a poor man, being as careful of the finances of the country as of his own purse. He reduced taxation, but his reforms were cheeseparing and ephemeral. He was fond of art and science, enriched the

Royal Library with many precious manuscripts, and was a member of the Academy; but his literary efforts have long since perished. He was neither a great prelate, a great Minister, nor a great man, but he was in a measure sincere and honest, when honesty and sincerity were singularly rare.

In 1717, when Fleury was still Bishop of Fréjus, Victor Amadeus, Duke of Savoy, came to that town on his way to the siege of Toulon. He said to the Bishop, 'I shall die or take Toulon.' Fleury replied, 'I shall lift up my hands to God, and pray that neither event may happen.' Towards the end of his life he almost fell into dotage. One day in mid-winter, being at a loss how to spend his time, he had a small altar erected in his garden, where some visitors found him performing his devotions in spite of the frost. 'You are risking your life by doing this,' they said. 'Pah!' he replied, 'you gentlemen are too soft.' His vigorous constitution, however, was not proof against the severity of the weather. He caught a cold, and died soon afterwards from its effects.

Cardinal Bernis was a genuine product of the age—clever, accomplished, and amiable, but shallow, artificial, and profligate. He entered the Church early in life, but though he belonged to a great and ancient family, he had no influential relatives or friends to assist him in obtaining preferment. When young, poor, and unknown he

Cardinal Bernis, 1715-1794.

called on Cardinal Fleury and begged for a benefice, but the old Minister knew that the Abbé's
conduct had been anything but clerical, so he
curtly told him, 'You have nothing to hope
for from me.'   'Then I shall wait,' replied
Bernis ; and he had not very long to wait.
He wielded a facile pen, and the pretty verses
he wrote brought him to the notice of Madame
de Pompadour, who gave him a pension and a
room at the Tuileries.   Through her favour he
was appointed Ambassador at Venice, in which
capacity he revealed such considerable ability
that he was appointed Minister for Foreign
Affairs, but he quarrelled with the omnipotent
favourite and was dismissed.   After her death
he was raised to the Cardinalate, and sent as
Ambassador to Rome, where he remained until
he died.   Voltaire, who appreciated Bernis and
his poems at their true worth, called him, ' Babet
la Bouquetière.'

Duc de Choiseul, 1719-1785. The Duc de Choiseul was a statesman of a
higher class than either Fleury or Bernis, but,
like the latter, he owed his first appointment
to the favour of Madame de Pompadour.   He
was made Ambassador in Vienna, succeeded
Bernis as Minister for Foreign Affairs, and subsequently became War Minister.   He introduced
many useful reforms, and by his foreign policy
he raised France, to some extent, from the
position of ignominy into which she had sunk.
But the State was too rotten to be susceptible of

any thorough repair by such measures as Choiseul adopted. He shared the errors of his order, but he was a high-minded gentleman, and refused to associate with Madame du Barry. For this he was dismissed from office, and as he still systematically treated the favourite with undisguised contempt, he was ultimately banished from Paris. On the death of Louis XV. he reappeared at Court to pay his respects to Louis XVI. and Marie Antoinette, whose marriage he had suggested and negotiated. ' I shall never forget what you have done for my happiness,' the Queen said to him. ' And for that of the whole of France,' adroitly replied Choiseul. Louis XVI., however, would never employ him, as ill-natured gossip, to which the stupid young King gave credence, had accused Choiseul of having poisoned the Dauphin, the father of Louis XVI.

Of the great nobles of the reign of Louis XV. none played a more conspicuous part than the Duc de Richelieu. The Duc de Lévis, in his Memoirs, compares him to Alcibiades, and indeed they had much in common. Both were the spoilt children of fortune, both were handsome and had great mental gifts, both were brave but vain and superficial, both were extravagant and licentious. But Alcibiades died a tragic death at the age of forty-three ; Richelieu lived to be ninety-two, and died in his bed. Richelieu, therefore, lived through

Armand du Plessis, Duc de Richelieu, 1696-1788.

almost the whole of the eighteenth century. He sat on the lap of Madame de Maintenon, Louis XIV. made him a pet, he was the boon companion of Louis XV., he filled high office under Louis XVI., and had he lived one year more he would have witnessed the taking of the Bastille. There was not a distinguished personage with whom he did not associate ; there was not an important event in which he did not take part ; there was not an intrigue or a scandal with which he was not connected. Some of his contemporaries attained a great age ; Fleury lived to be ninety, Fontenelle a hundred, and Voltaire eighty-four. But Fleury was a churchman and statesman only, Fontenelle and Voltaire confined themselves to literature ; Richelieu was a man of all things. He went through every experience and had every opportunity of achieving the greatest celebrity. He filled the highest posts in the army, diplomacy, the internal administration of the country and at Court, and was an Academician as well. Two princesses of the blood royal quarrelled for his favour, and two great ladies fought a duel for his sake. He was sent three times to the Bastille ; he was wounded three times in the field ; he was married three times—the last time at the age of eighty-four ; he fought duels, killing two of his opponents ; he was the most accomplished, the wittiest, the most open-handed, the most gallant man of his age. He personified the eighteenth century, in short, as completely, if not more completely, than did Madame de Pompadour; but while Madame de Pompadour reflected its artistic grace and voluptuous charm, Richelieu embodied its vices, its frivolity, its scandalous levity, its superstitions, and base corruption, and so it was that the name he left was only that of a most successful Lothario. To some extent, however, his fame has been unjustly obscured, for the victory of Fontenoy was greatly due to him. He took Port Mahon and conquered Hanover, but the curse of the eighteenth century was on him and on all he did. He pillaged Hanover so shamefully that his own soldiers christened him 'Father Marauder.' With the spoils he built the Pavilion de Hanovre (which still stands in the Boulevards), adjoining the house of a lady whom he secretly visited by passing through a revolving mantelpiece.

When Governor of Guienne he displayed the most sumptuous hospitality, but he turned his palace into a gambling hell. Governors of provinces were called upon to act as umpires in 'affairs of honour.' One evening at Bordeaux, while he was at the opera, a young lieutenant inconsiderately rushed up to his box and said he had been insulted by a brother officer, who had spat in his face. 'Fie,' replied the Marshal, 'go and wash it.' When Ambassador at Vienna he brought his mission to a successful issue, but he was gravely compromised in 'a matter of sorcery,' in which the chief agent lost his life. The Academy, out of respect for the memory of his great-uncle, the Cardinal, elected him a member. The speech he delivered at his reception evoked much applause, but he had concocted it from a number of speeches with which Fontenelle and others had supplied him for the purpose. He had no hand in the introduction of Madame de Pompadour and Madame du Barry to the King, but he encouraged the King's fancies and assiduously courted the favour of the royal mistresses.

Madame de Pompadour had a daughter, a child of ten, for whom she was anxious to secure a husband of high rank. To Richelieu, who was then married to a Princess of Lorraine, she one day unexpectedly offered the hand of the young girl for his son, the Duc de Fronsac. Richelieu was not to be taken aback by the abruptness of the proposal, and quietly replied, 'I am overwhelmed by the honour you intend conferring on me, and only beg for time to consult the Empress Queen (Maria Theresa); her consent is required by one who has the advantage of being connected with the House of Lorraine.' Madame de Pompadour took the hint and looked out for another son-in-law; but the child died soon afterwards. Louis XV. bore him no grudge for his refusal of Madame de Pompadour's matrimonial overture, and gave him a lifelong friendship. He accompanied the King one day to hear a famous preacher, who, with singular courage and zeal, had fulminated against the vices and scandals of the Court. 'Marshal,' said Louis XV., 'the preacher threw a good many stones into your garden.' 'Sire,' replied Richelieu, 'did not some also fall into your Majesty's park?'

He showed as little concern about the conduct of the ladies to whom he was married as he expected them to show for his conduct. He happened on one occasion to find his wife conversing rather too familiarly with his equerry. 'Fancy, madame,' he calmly said, 'how awkward you would have felt had any one else but myself come into the room!' When this lady died he wooed the daughter of the Prince de Guise. The engagement was still a secret when the same equerry, believing that Richelieu had forgiven him, called and begged the Marshal to take him back into his service. 'How did you know,' asked the Marshal, 'that I was going to get married again?'

He was never on friendly terms with Louis XVI. and Marie Antoinette; still he was often at Court, and Louis XVI. asked him one day what public opinion thought of the reigns of his predecessors compared with his own. 'Sire,' replied the veteran courtier, 'under Louis XIV. no one dared utter a word, under Louis XV. they whispered, under your Majesty they talk aloud.'

The Fermiers-Generaux and financiers of

France played a very conspicuous but not very reputable part in the history of the eighteenth century. They suffered, however, to some extent, unjustly for the evils of a system for which they were not directly responsible, and which was bound up with the intricate fiscal organisation of the country. By that system, which was established in 1697, and lasted until the Revolution, the collection of some of the principal taxes of the kingdom was farmed to a company of Fermiers-Generaux. They contracted to provide the Treasury with a stated sum, and were entitled to appropriate as their profit all the money they gathered over that amount. The sum which they were called upon to return to the Treasury from their 'farms' was varied according to the yield of the taxes from year to year, and was increased at different times during the century.

In the earlier part of the eighteenth century many of the financiers sprang from the lower, if not the lowest, classes of society, and were unfitted by birth and education for the great position they held—a position, it was said, they achieved by ill-gotten gains and the plunder of the State. They were, however, an outcome of the age; many of the highest in the land were no freer from its taints, and were equally reckless and abandoned in their lives. Instead of conciliating public opinion by making a good use of their wealth, the Fermiers-Generaux and their associates indulged in the most wanton extravagance and licentiousness, thus exposing themselves to the envy and the scorn of the people. And yet the nobles who scoffed at the 'upstarts,' and loudly applauded the plays in which they were held up to ridicule and opprobrium, still secretly entered into partnership with them—as did even Louis XV. himself— and readily enough married their daughters, as was said at the time, 'to manure their lands or re-gild their escutcheons.' Louis XV., talking to the Duc de Noailles, praised the fiscal system, saying that the Fermiers-Generaux 'sustained' France: 'Yes, sire,' replied the Duke, 'as the rope sustains the hanged.' Many of them, however,—especially those who flourished in the second part of the eighteenth century— were men of honour, high attainments, and great deserts; but the worthy had to suffer with the unworthy, and in 1794 the Revolution saw thirty-five Fermiers-Generaux sent to the guillotine whose only crime was that they had succeeded to the office of their predecessors.

Paul Poisson de Bourvalais, who was born in the latter part of the seventeenth century, was a type of his class, and his life affords an interesting illustration of the chequered career of a financier of the day. He was the son of an agricultural labourer, left his native Brittany in his teens, was first a servant of the future Fermier-General Thenevin, and afterwards became a clerk to a

Paul Poisson de Bourvalais, † 1719.

timber merchant.   This place, however, he soon
threw up, and returning to his native village,
was appointed a bailiff.   It happened that M. de
Pontchartrin, first President of the Parlement
of Rennes, and subsequently Chancellor of France,
came across young Poisson, and being favourably impressed by his engaging appearance and
manner, asked him in the course of conversation
what the document was that he held in his hand.
It happened to be a writ, and the President was
struck by the way in which it was drawn up.
'It is a pity,' said M. de Pontchartrin, 'that
you should carry on this poor trade.   Come
and see me, and I shall do something for you.'
Poisson at once followed his heaven-sent patron
to Paris, where he was soon appointed an over-
seer.   To qualify for admittance into more
exalted spheres, he affixed the title of 'de Bourvalais' to his plebeian name, and by his intelligence and great capacity for work, aided by M.
de Pontchartrin's patronage, he soon succeeded
in obtaining employment at the War Office and
a share in the contracts for army stores.   In
time he filled twelve high offices ; he became
Secretary to the Council, and Secretary to the
King, while in addition he had the conduct of
a bewildering mass of business, all of which he
transacted himself.   His wealth grew to be
enormous, his town house was a palace, and his
château the rendezvous of all that was fashionable.   Then it was that he met his former

master, M. Thenevin, who, being envious of the success of his ex-servant, referred sneeringly to his earlier life, and wound up by saying in an aggravating tone, 'Come, you must confess that at one time you were my lacquey.' 'That is so,' replied Bourvalais, 'but had you been a lacquey, you would have been one to this day.'

Fortune, however, after smiling on Bourvalais for many years, suddenly jilted him. The Regent was in financial straits; financiers and Fermiers-Generaux were a legitimate prey, and could be squeezed with impunity. In 1716 a number of them were charged with fraud, their books were seized and examined, and they were, as a matter of course, convicted. Bourvalais suffered with the rest. His property was confiscated, and he was imprisoned for two years. His property was then returned to him, but he was mulcted in a fine of 4,400,000 francs. The strain of the anxiety and privations he had undergone, however, proved too much for his health, and he died almost immediately after his release from prison in 1719.

Samuel Bernard, the son of a painter, came into public notice in consequence of a peculiar incident in his career. At the time of the War of the Succession the notion of bleeding the Fermiers-Generaux had not yet obtained, and it was thought to appeal for help to the great financier in a manner likely to ensure success. So one day the whole of Paris rang with the news that

Samuel Bernard, 1651-1739.

Samuel Bernard had been received at Marly, and most graciously spoken to by the Grand Monarque, with whom he had walked alone in the gardens for a quarter of an hour. The result of the interview was the offer of a loan, which his Majesty deigned to accept. Later on, Louis XV. sent an application to him for a few millions, but received the reply, 'When something is wanted from one, the least that can be done is to ask one for it in person.' He attained his purpose. He was presented to the King, kindly received, shown over the palace, and though made fun of by the Court, he at once sent the money. The Marquis de Favière, a man noted for never repaying what he borrowed, called on Bernard one day and said to him, 'I am going to astonish you greatly. I am not acquainted with you, and I ask you to lend me 500 louis.' 'I shall astonish you still more,' said Bernard, 'I *do* know you, and I shall lend you the money.' Bernard was superstitious, and imagined that his life depended on that of a certain black hen, and, strangely enough, it is related that they both died on the same day.

The literature of the eighteenth century is now neglected in comparison with that of the seventeenth. The works of the great classics Corneille, Racine, Molière, Lafontaine, and some others are still widely read ; but only scholars or students read much of Voltaire, beyond, perhaps, his 'Siècle de Louis XIV.,' his 'Charles

XII.,' and perhaps an occasional chapter of the 'Dictionnaire Philosophique.' Of Rousseau, who, it must be borne in mind, was not a Frenchman, 'The Confessions' are read, though from motives presently to be referred to; while from curiosity one may peep into the 'Contrat Social,' but his 'Emile,' which revolutionised society, is obsolete, and the 'Nouvelle Héloise,' which caused a fever of excitement among the cultured classes at the time of its publication, is regarded as morbid and unwholesome food which only the most robust stomach can digest. Many explanations could be given of the scant courtesy shown to the literary productions of the eighteenth century, despite the fact that they brimmed over with wit, dealt in a masterly fashion with every subject they touched, and enchanted, indeed almost turned, the heads of the people.

The writers of the seventeenth century became classics because they grappled boldly and in a large spirit with moral and economic problems which affected not only their own generation, but continue to affect succeeding generations as well; and because they treated of those human passions which are common to all ages and to all climes. The men of letters of the eighteenth century, as a rule, discussed merely the social, political, and philosophical questions of their own day, and of the French nation only. They wrote with special objects in view, and for certain conditions of life, which have ceased to exist. For a time they wielded a far greater influence than did their predecessors. Voltaire and Rousseau were buried in the Pantheon, and had posthumous honours offered to them which never fell to the share of Corneille and Molière ; but when their purpose had been achieved, and the conditions had passed away for which they had written, their ashes were removed from the Pantheon, and their works fell into comparative neglect.

But though this is true of most of the once standard works of the eighteenth century, the memoirs and letters of that period are still a source of unceasing delight. They were—perhaps unconsciously—written for all time. Their style is exquisite, they are replete with information concerning the history, politics, and customs of the period ; moreover, they gratify a weakness common to most people by admitting the reader into the private life, into the innermost recesses of the mind and the heart of the great. For these reasons we even now pore over Rousseau's ' Confessions.' The memoirs of Madame d'Epinay, of Madame d'Oberkirch, and of the Comte de Ségur, to mention only a few examples, are still universally read. But for their memoirs Marmontel would be classed with Colardeau, Collé with Dorat, and D'Argenson with the Cardinal de Polignac. Its ' esprit '—wit, sarcasm, cleverness, taste, gracefulness of expression, and lightness of style, all of which help to constitute the word ' esprit '—was the distinctive trait of the eighteenth century. By it the salons won their fame, but for it the many conversations that were held in the salons would not have been preserved for our enjoyment. It was for that 'esprit' Voltaire was invited to Berlin and Diderot to St. Petersburg, and that Grimm became the correspondent of the crowned heads of Europe. But literature in a measure suffered from the all-pervading tone, for that tone was the result of the spirit and the fashions of the day, and was equally transient and evanescent.

Fontenelle, the nephew of Corneille, was the contemporary of Racine and Boileau, who quarrelled with him for presuming to criticise their works, and of Voltaire, who called him his 'Parent d'esprit.' A prolific writer, a poet, a satirist, a mathematician, and a philosopher, his chief claim to celebrity was that he treated the most abstruse subjects clearly and without pedantry—a gift which enabled him to popularise science to an extent hitherto unknown. 'You know how to make things agreeable,' wrote Voltaire, 'which other philosophers can hardly make intelligible. Nature owed such a man to France, who can instruct the scholar while giving the ignorant a taste for science.' To the end of his long life Fontenelle was highly esteemed for his conversation and wit. The salon he most frequented was that of Helvetius, a financier and philosopher. Helvetius, to celebrate his marriage with

Bernard le Bouvier de Fontenelle, 1657-1757.

Mademoiselle de Ligneville, the daughter of a Lorraine magnate and a relation of Marie Antoinette, gave a banquet, at which Fontenelle was among the guests. After having profusely complimented his hostess, Fontenelle, in a fit of abstraction, passed before her into the dining-room. 'How,' she asked, 'am I to value your compliments—you pass on without even looking at me!' 'Had I looked at you,' replied the old philosopher, 'I should not have passed on.' He was a bachelor, and very fond of society—in fact, was so well known for his social proclivities that when his body was being conveyed to its last resting-place, Piron, on meeting the funeral, remarked, 'This is the first time that M. de Fontenelle is not leaving his house to dine out.' A philosopher to the end, he preserved a perfect composure even in his last agony. 'You suffer!' said his physician to him. 'No,' replied Fontenelle, 'I only find it difficult to exist.' These were his last words. Fontenelle's writings have vanished into space with the progress of science and learning, but the recollection of his popularity remains, though it is somewhat dimmed by his great egotism. He had the reputation of being callous and heartless, though in reality he was charitable and kind, and could well say of himself, 'I have never turned any virtue, however small, into ridicule.'

'Which sovereign do you most dread?'

Voltaire

some one asked Frederick the Great. 'King Voltaire,' he replied. To give an adequate *François Arouet de Voltaire,* notion of the intellectual sovereignty that Voltaire exercised during his long life, or a correct *1694-1778.* idea of the man, one would require to be intimately acquainted with the entire history of the eighteenth century, to be saturated with the spirit of the age and the tone of its society, to be conversant with all its literature and the drift of its moral and philosophical forces. It would require, in addition, a thorough knowledge of Voltaire's works and correspondence, and of his life, both public and private. This task has baffled the skill and ingenuity of most of his biographers, but its very diversity and complexity still induce writers to attempt it. French writers, however, of late have been content to single out for treatment special portions of his works or periods of his career. These necessarily present an incomplete picture. Voltaire in his youth —the Voltaire who was Madame de Pompadour's courtier, the Duc de Villars's visitor at Vaux and Adrienne Lecouvreur's friend, the Voltaire who was caned by the lacqueys of the Chevalier de Rohan for having dared to contradict him, sent to the Bastille for presuming to remonstrate, and who then fled to England—was a different man from the Voltaire who lived at King Stanislas' court at Luneville, the lover of Madame de Chatelet, and the guest of Frederick the Great. A very different man still was the patriarch of Ferney, and a totally distinct personage was the Voltaire who, when past eighty years of age, after having been imprisoned, outlawed, and reviled, received in Paris an ovation the like of which few sovereigns ever enjoyed.

Even greater contrasts still appear in a character in which the most bitter malignity was blended with the sincerest sympathy. He pursued his literary adversaries with unrelenting hate, while he pleaded for the rehabilitation of the memory of Calas, of La Barre, of Lally Tollendal. He detested Rousseau and loved Diderot. He went to law with the President de Brosses because of some trifling dispute over property, yet he munificently endowed the great-niece of Corneille. He inveighed against the Church, and built churches ; he was at the head of the philosophical—in modern words— the democratic movement of the day, and he wrote panegyrics of Louis XIV. and the Regent. But contradictory as all this seems, Voltaire was always true to himself, true to his common sense, his good taste, to his abhorrence of despotism, with its consequent injustice, and true, above all, to liberty.[1] He was not yet of age when he was sent to durance vile in the Bastille. His scathing wit had gained him a bad name, and

[1] See 'Le Roi Voltaire,' by Arsène Houssaye, and 'Life of Voltaire,' by Saint-Marc Girardin.

matters were brought to a climax when he published, though anonymously, a poem on the late King Louis XIV., which ended with the line : 'I have seen these woes, and I am not twenty.'[1] After his release from the prison to which he had been sent by the Regent, he was hospitably welcomed by the Prince, whom he thanked with the words, 'Sir, I should be well pleased were his Majesty henceforth to provide me with my victuals, but I beg your Highness no longer to provide me with lodgings.'

At the age of ten Voltaire had begun to write poems which attracted the attention of his schoolmaster. At sixteen he declared to his father that he would follow no other profession but that of a man of letters. At twenty-one he began the 'Henriade,' and at twenty-two he brought out, at the Français, his first tragedy, 'Œdipus,' which at once gave him a leading place among the dramatists of the day. From his earliest youth he was indefatigable with his pen, and at all periods of his life, whether a prisoner in the Bastille, a gay young man of fashion, or weighed down with years, he devoted part of every day to writing. He wrote with great fluency, but never spared the pruning-knife, being well aware how much easier it is to reduce than to add. A friend who called one day was surprised at the number of reams of paper he had filled. 'Why

---

[1] 'J'ai vu ces maux, et je n'ai pas vingt ans.'

do you write at such length?' he inquired.
'Because I have no time to write briefly,'
answered Voltaire.

He was accused of religious scepticism and
impiety. He had a horror of cant and hypocrisy, he had an equal horror of the bigoted
intolerance of the clergy, which corresponded so
ill with the corruption and the profligacy of
many leading Churchmen, but by exposing
their vices with scathing irony, he drew on
himself the anathemas of the Church. His
was the phrase, 'If God did not exist he would
have to be invented,' which are scarcely the
words of an atheist. But he was a scoffer, and
could never restrain a joke at the expense of
religious belief. When walking one day with
Piron they passed a priest carrying the Host, and
Voltaire raised his hat. 'I see,' said Piron,
'that you have become reconciled with each
other.' 'Not altogether ; we exchange greet-
ings, but we do not speak,' answered Voltaire.
Once, on a very cold evening at school, he
asked his playfellows to make way for him in
front of the fire. 'If you do not go away,' he
said, 'I shall send you to get warm with Pluto.'
'Say hell at once,' replied the boy, 'it is warmer
there.' 'Pah!' exclaimed young Arouet, 'I am
not more certain of the existence of the one than
of the other.' This reply might have cost him
dear had it come to the knowledge of the Church.
In the following year Father Legay, irritated

by some remark the boy had made, took hold
of him by the collar and exclaimed, 'Unfortunate youth, you will some day raise the banner
of deism in France!' He could not have
known how true his prophecy was to prove.
Voltaire always had a Bible on his desk, and
when a friend asked him why, seeing the
opinions he professed, the sacred volume was
lying there; 'Because,' replied Voltaire, 'those
who are framing an indictment should always
have the case of their adversaries at hand.'
On another occasion, at a party, the antiquity
of the world was being discussed, and, being
asked his opinion on the subject, he said, 'As
for me, I believe the world is like an old flirt
who dissembles her age.'

After his second incarceration in the Bastille,
which lasted only a few days, he was banished
at his own request to England, preferring the
fogs of the Thames to the walls of a dungeon.
He remained three years in London and its
neighbourhood, going into society under the
patronage of Lords Bolingbroke, Peterborough,
Hervey, and Bath, studying English philosophy
and literature, and frequenting the houses of the
great authors of the day. He seems not to
have hit it off with Congreve. Voltaire wished
merely to do honour to the man of letters,
whereas Congreve took his visit as a tribute to his
social position, and received him very grandly.
'Were you merely a gentleman,' said Voltaire

meaningly, ' I should not have had the pleasure of coming to you to-day.'

He knew Pope, Swift, Steele, Gay, and Young, and once, speaking to the latter about Milton's ' Paradise Lost,' he referred to the passage on Sin and Death as ' a disgusting and abominable story,' to which Young replied by extemporising the following lines :—

> You are so witty, so profligate, and thin,
> At once we think you Milton, death, and sin.

He took advantage of his exile to learn English, and it was fortunate for him that he did so.   Though France and England were then at peace there was not much love lost between the peoples of the two countries.   He was walking in the streets of London one day, when the mob, seeing a Frenchman, set upon him, and would have handled him very roughly had he not climbed on a post and placated them with a speech, beginning, ' Worthy Britons, I was unfortunate enough not to have been born one of you,'—whereupon the mob cheered him lustily and carried him home in triumph.   But despite his long stay in England, his mind was too thoroughly French to be deeply im- pressed with English literature, and Shakespeare's plays especially seem not to have excited his admiration.   ' Hamlet,' in particular, was an ob- ject of derision to him.   Nevertheless he made use of 'Julius Cæsar' for one of his tragedies, and to an English acquaintance who expressed his regret that Shakespeare was so little appreciated in France, he replied, 'Yes, Shakespeare is only known here in translation, in which the defects remain and the beauties are lost. A man who is born blind cannot imagine that a rose is lovely when his fingers are only pricked by its thorns.'

He was well aware how much the success of a performance depended upon the manner in which the comedians realised the meaning of their parts, and was most energetic in rehearsing with them. When 'Merope' was being rehearsed, he complained that the principal actress, Madame Dusmenil, did not throw enough warmth and force into the delivery of her lines. 'One must have the very devil in one,' she replied, 'to reach the high pitch you require.' 'Yes, yes,' he answered, 'that is so ; one must have the devil in one to excel in any branch of art ; unless one has the devil in one, one can neither be a good poet nor a good comedian.' 'Merope' was brilliantly acted, and turned out a great success. The author, as he alleged in later years,[1] was embraced by the Duchesse de Villars, from whose box he witnessed the performance, and was called several times before the curtain. His triumph made Fontenelle jealous. 'The performers,' he said, 'do Voltaire

[1] 'Correspondance de Voltaire.'

much credit, but the play itself does Madame Dusmenil more credit still.' Fontenelle's sarcasm was not justified, for of Voltaire's numerous plays 'Merope' is one of the best, and still holds the stage.

He was too conscious of his merits to ape humility, but though it cannot be said that he ever erred on the side of modesty, he detested fulsome and silly compliments. At Ferney, where he was overwhelmed with visitors from every country in Europe, anxious to make the acquaintance of one of the greatest men of the century, an inopportune sightseer, having lavished on him the most extravagant praise, said, 'I come to contemplate the light of the world,' whereupon Voltaire turned round to his niece, Madame Denis, and said, 'Quick! madame, please bring me a pair of snuffers.'

Great men have their foibles, and Voltaire was no exception to the rule. It was his dearest wish to ingratiate himself with the King, but though he was made a Gentleman of the Bed-chamber, and enjoyed Madame de Pompadour's friendship, he never succeeded in obtaining a footing at Court. To please him, and at the same time to flatter the King, Madame de Pompadour requested the poet to write a play in honour of the victories of Louis XV., giving due prominence to the part of the royal hero. The play—a ballet called the 'Temple of Glory' —was performed at Versailles by members of the Court. Madame de Pompadour appeared as the Goddess of Glory, and an actor impersonated the Emperor Trajan, intended to be Louis XV. In the last scene the goddess approached the Emperor and led him into the Temple of National Felicity. Etiquette being suspended for the occasion, Voltaire, to his infinite joy, was a guest in the royal box, and was so elated by the success of his work that he embraced the King, asking, 'Trajan, do you recognise yourself?' The attendants rushed forward and seized the bold enthusiast, but Trajan magnanimously pardoned him. By this uncourtierlike action Voltaire spoiled the best chance he had ever had of gaining the favour of his sovereign.

Voltaire was always funny. Jean Baptiste Rousseau, the greatest poet then living, read to him his 'Ode to Posterity,' and asked him what he thought of it. 'It is an ode which will never reach its address,' observed Voltaire, showing an accurate prevision of its fate. Again, when a member of the Academy of Chalons boasted before him of the many claims of that body, saying 'it was the eldest daughter of the French Academy,' 'Most certainly,' was his answer, 'she is a good girl, and will never get herself talked about.' Shortly before his death in Paris, Fariau de St. Ange, the translator of Ovid's 'Metamorphoses,' called to pay his respects, and, wishing to give an original turn

Jean Baptiste Rousseau, 1671-1741.

to his compliment, said, 'To-day I have only come to see Homer; to-morrow I shall return to see Euripides and Sophocles, then Tacitus and then Lucian.' 'I am very old, sir,' pleaded Voltaire, 'could you not pay all the visits in one day?' About the same time Franklin presented his grandson to the old philosopher, and begged him to bless the child. 'God and Liberty,' said Voltaire, 'is the only suitable blessing for the grandson of Franklin.' Among the crowd of visitors he had at this time was Turgot, who, suffering severely from gout, had to be carried into the room. 'How are you, M. Turgot?' inquired Voltaire. 'I am in great pain and hardly able to walk,' replied Turgot. 'Whenever I see M. Turgot,' said Voltaire excitedly to the company, 'I think of Nebuchadnezzar!' 'Ah, but with feet of clay!' returned Turgot. 'But with a head of gold; yes, with a head of gold!' rejoined Voltaire.

Diderot,
1712-1784.
Diderot is beyond the scope of a sketch. An elaborate biography would hardly do justice to this extraordinary man. His genius and versatility brought every subject within their range. There was nothing too lofty for him to conceive or elucidate, nothing, however trivial, that was not ennobled by his touch; and whatever he took up he worked at passionately and with unflagging perseverance. He was a philologist and a bookseller's hack, a poet

and a pamphleteer, a musician and an art critic,
a geometrician and a dramatist, an indefatigable
correspondent and a magnificent talker, a profound philosopher and a fashionable novelist.
His robust constitution fortunately enabled him
to meet all demands—those of the public for his
writings, those of his friends for his society.   In
influencing the progress of thought, its develop-
ments and effect, he was second only to Voltaire,
but Voltaire was always in prosperous circumstances, while Diderot was always poor.   He had
a family to maintain, and he maintained them,
though he was a gambler, an art collector, and a
spendthrift.   Though needy and always busy—
for twenty years he toiled at the thirty volumes
of the 'Encyclopædia'—he helped those who
were in greater need, with his money or his pen.
A hairdresser once asked him to compose an
advertisement for some wonderful hair-restorer,
and Diderot instantly complied with the request.
On another occasion a lady in distressed circumstances begged him to indite a letter in her
name to the Duc de la Vrilliére, who had
forsaken her.   'Sit down,' he said ; 'let us see
what we can do.'   He wrote—'Sir—As long as
I lived upon the gifts which your affection for
me prompted you to make, I forbore from
appealing to you, but of the proofs of our
former love all I have left is your portrait, and
that I shall soon have to sell for bread.'   The
result of this appeal was that the Duke sent the

lady fifty louis. Some years later she called again, and on this occasion she implored Diderot to obtain her admission to a hospital. Diderot again wrote to the Duke, and was again successful. But, kind and sympathetic as he was, he had no patience with simpletons. Talking of a man who belonged to that class of persons who are indiscriminately officious and good-natured to all comers, he said, 'He is one of those fools who carries his kindness about with him as a tree carries apples, without wishing to do so, and without any consciousness of the fact.'

His mental activity was prodigious, he wrote enormously and well, but he excelled in conversation. All those who knew him were entranced by his eloquence and intensity, his spontaneity, the fiery impetuosity of his mind, the originality of his wit, and the charm of his manner. When talking to the Empress Catherine he was so carried away by his ardour that he familiarly put his hand on her knee, but she only smiled, and the conversation proceeded. One day, in one of his disputes with the Empress on philosophy, he said that he argued with her at a disadvantage. 'Fie! is there any difference between men?' replied her Majesty, who wished to be considered possessed of intelligence on a par with his own. To assist Diderot the Empress purchased his library, but allowed him to retain it until his death; moreover, she employed him to acquire for her a collection of works of art. Amongst the pictures he bought for his august patron were those of Baron Thiers, who had just died. While the negotiations were progressing he was brought in contact with one of the Baron's heirs, the Maréchal de Broglie. The Marshal's brother, a mischievous wag, wishing to make fun of Diderot, who always wore black clothes, asked whether he was in mourning for Russia. 'Had I to wear mourning for a nation,' he replied, 'I should not have to go so far.' He might almost indeed have worn mourning for the French nation, for the Revolution was at its door. Though he could not have foreseen its excesses and crimes—which he would have been one of the first to deplore—he helped to accelerate its coming. No one exposed more vividly than he the abuses and the intolerance of the clergy, and the absolutism of the governing classes. In this respect he resembled Voltaire, but he went further than Voltaire. He was nearly an atheist. He had no religious scruples, though at the end of his life he gave expression to some feeling of belief ; and he was no courtier, and had no cravings for social honours. 'Dear me,' said the Maréchal de Castries, whose aristocratic pride was irritated by the importance the philosophers had gained in the eyes of the public, 'wherever I go I hear every one talking of this fellow Diderot and that fellow Rousseau, mere nobodies, who possess no house of their own, and lodge on a third floor. Truly it is impossible for one to accustom oneself to such things.' Diderot required no house of his own, he was lodged in the admiration of millions of his countrymen.

Alexis Piron, 1689-1773.

Alexis Piron, a native of Dijon, began life as a copyist, and was employed in that capacity by a wealthy and conceited financier. 'You will only have to copy the verses I write,' his patron told him. 'The task will be easy if the verses are good,' replied Piron. 'I should think they are good—they are by me!' was the self-satisfied rejoinder. Piron, however, thought otherwise, left his Crœsus for the Bar, but soon tired of its drudgery, and became a dramatic author. His plays were acted in the best theatres in Paris, and were very successful; but only one, 'The Métromanie,' has kept the stage. When his last play was in rehearsal the company requested him to make some alterations, pointing out that Voltaire always considered suggestions from them. Piron, whose head had been turned by his success, refused, saying, 'Voltaire works in mosaics, I cast in bronze.' The play proved a complete fiasco. He was elected to the Academy, but he had written a grossly indecent ode in his early youth, an error which was always being thrown in his face, and pursued him to the end of his life. Louis XV., who was not precisely squeamish, refused to sanction his election because of this poem. Madame de Pompadour was more liberal, and gave him a pension. It may have been a case of sour grapes, but Piron never lost an opportunity of having a fling at the Academy. Walking past the Louvre with a friend, he said, 'Mark, there sits the French Academy; there are forty of them with the wit of four.' And in the same vein he composed his own epitaph : 'Here lies Piron, who was nothing—not even an Academician.'[1]

His celebrity and popularity came to him through his wit. He went to Brussels to see Jean Baptiste Rousseau, who had been banished from France for his calumnious attacks on living authors. Rousseau was a species of literary Janus, who, to please all sections of the community, wrote deeply devotional works for the one, and extremely licentious ones for the other. They were walking together in the country when the church bells in the distance rang the Angelus. Rousseau went down on his knees. 'Do not put yourself to this unnecessary trouble,' said Piron, 'God alone sees us.' One night at the play he kept looking rather hard at his neighbour, a lady of questionable reputation. She suddenly said, 'Have you regarded me long enough?'—to which he answered, 'Madame, I look at you, but I do not regard you!' Once, however, he caught a tartar. He was asked

---

[1] 'Ci-gît Piron, qui fut rien—pas même Academicien.'

at a party if he could tell the difference between a woman and a mirror. 'A woman,' he replied, 'talks without reflecting, a mirror reflects without talking.' Upon this a lady asked, 'Can you now, M. Piron, tell me the difference between a man and a mirror?' And as Piron remained silent she went on, 'A mirror is always polished, while a man's manners sometimes are not.'

Claude Henri de Fusée, Abbé de Voisenon, 1708-1775.
The Abbé de Voisenon was one of that great pleiad of poets who flitted across the horizon of the eighteenth century, charming their contemporaries with pretty and ephemeral verses. He had been invited to dinner by the Prince de Conti, but forgot his engagement, and when, later on, the Abbé came to pay his respects to the Prince the latter turned his back on him. 'I am glad to perceive,' said the Abbé, 'that your Highness is not angry with me, for, sir, you are not in the habit of turning your back to your enemies.'

Marquis de Bièvre, 1747-1789.
The Marquis de Bièvre was famous for his puns, which were collected and published. Puns unfortunately cannot be translated, and but one example of his gift can be quoted. Louis XV., to whom the peculiar accomplishment of M. de Bièvre had been reported, commanded him to his presence and said to him, 'I hear that you make jokes on every subject—well, make one on me.' 'Your Majesty,' replied the Marquis, bowing most deferentially, 'is not a subject.'

Some reference must be made to the comedians who played a considerable part in the social history of the French eighteenth century. In England the stage reached a high degree of eminence long before it did so in France. 'Othello' and 'Hamlet' were performed in London when gross farces and pantomimes were the chief attraction of the Paris stage. Charles II. patronised the drama as much as. Louis XIV., and the names of the many comedians who delighted English audiences in the eighteenth century can readily be recalled. In England, however, the theatre was not a universal resource and pastime, nor a royal institution ; it had no hold on the imagination, and did not enter into the daily thoughts of the people : and with some few notable exceptions, society closed its doors to those who made it their profession. In France from the early middle ages play-going was general throughout the country. Towards the end of the fifteenth century the old Passion Plays were superseded by profane ones, which were given at Court and elsewhere, chiefly imported from Italy, and unless translated, were acted by Italians. During the Civil War in England Corneille's plays were performed before Richelieu, and during the Restoration, when the drama in England was in its decay, Molière and Racine produced their masterpieces before Louis XIV. In 1658 Molière and his company obtained from the Duc d'Orleans the privilege of styling themselves 'Comédiens de Monsieur.' The following year Louis XIV. secured the privileges of the opera by statute, and allowed it to establish Academies of Music in Paris and the provinces. Two years later an opera was performed for the first time in a house called 'The Royal Academy of Music,' and Lulli, the composer, was made a noble as early as 1672. Molière's former company was now styled 'Comédiens de la Troupe du Roi,' but some years previously Louis XIV. had founded the 'Théâtre Français' by royal charter. It was subsidised by the King, and placed under the control of his highest Court functionaries. It is true there was no French counterpart of Nell Gwynne to found a ducal line, but during the whole of the eighteenth century actors and actresses were as great people in their way as the statesmen or the titled favourites of the sovereign. Every leading singer, actress, or dancer was taken up by some grandee or man of fashion who wished to be considered in the vogue. Her dresses, diamonds, and chariots, her house and her entertainments were the talk of the town. If she was clever and accomplished her salon was a focus of attraction. Magnates and men of letters were her friends and companions, and as literary men—some from the fact of their being Academicians—had a higher social position than literary men had in England, the comedians borrowed some of their prestige. The French public interested itself in the stage and all connected with it far more than the English. It was more critical, more enthusiastic, more emotional and demonstrative, more in unison with the performers, who were not mere puppets in a show, not mummers only. A brilliant actor or actress became the darling of the world, of the mob and society alike.

The actor Darbeval, being sued for debt, threatened to leave Paris. Madame du Barry opened a subscription on his behalf, which in a couple of days rose to ninety thousand francs; and when Molé fell ill, Louis XV. sent twice to inquire after his health. The Duc de Richelieu presented him with a costume worth eleven thousand francs, and the Baron d'Oppéde gave one worth eighteen thousand francs to the actor Fleury. Adrienne Lecouvreur was so overwhelmed with invitations that she could not respond to them all; Madame St. Huberty, the singer, while on a tour, arrived at Marseilles by sea in a gorgeous gondola, clothed in an antique costume, rowed by oarsmen who were similarly clad. When she landed, amid a display of fireworks, she received a public ovation. Later on she married the Comte d'Entraigues, with whom she was assassinated in London in 1812.

Mademoiselle Clairon, the tragedienne, was the first actress who wore antique dress in classical parts instead of appearing in powder and

Mdlle. Clairon, 1723-1803.

hoops, as was the general custom ; she was also the first to speak in a natural voice instead of the accepted style of ranting declamation. She had the Court at her feet ; Voltaire wrote hymns in her praise ; princesses, even the austere Madame Necker, were her friends. Her success turned her head.   At a State concert she happened to be seated next to a duchess, who disdainfully said, ' Honest women should wear badges to distinguish them.' ' Then you would wish,' replied Clairon, ' to give the public a chance of seeing how few there are.'   On one occasion, to spite a rival actress, she prevented a new play from being performed when the house was already full.   There was a scene, and she was sent to prison for this act of insubordination.   When the police officer came to arrest her she told him, ' I am ready to obey the King's orders ; all I have is the King's—my fortune, my person, and my life, all but my honour, which remains intact.' ' True,' replied the facetious official, ' where there is nothing the King loses his rights.'   Bad health obliged her to leave the stage when still in her prime.   The young Margrave of Baireuth, who had known her in Paris, invited her to his castle, where she filled the part of his Madame de Maintenon for seventeen years.   She then had to make way for Lady Craven, whom the Margrave married after the death of his wife, a Princess of Coburg.   Clairon returned to Paris, lived there through the Revolution, and died in obscurity at the age of eighty.

Perhaps of all the stage idols of the public, Vestris, the dancer, the founder of the 'illustrious' house of that name, was the vainest. A lady walking in the gardens of the Palais Royal one morning inadvertently stepped on his toe. ' I beg your pardon, sir,' she said, 'I hope you are not hurt.' ' No, madame,' he replied, ' you have not hurt me, but you had very nearly put the whole of Paris in mourning for a fortnight.'

Mademoiselle Guimard, a dancer, and the plainest of her profession, was all the fashion. Princes, bishops, and financiers beggared themselves for her. She had a palace in town and a château in the country, where the greatest ladies elbowed women of her own calling in a gay throng. After a performance at Court the King settled a pension of 1500 francs on her. 'I accept it,' she said contemptuously, ' because of the donor, but it is hardly enough to pay the wages of the man who snuffs my candles.'

Mdlle. Guimard, 1743-1816.

The Comédiens du Roi were often ordered to act at Court, and were in constant relations with the Court and its satellites. But these great personages were not content with the passive enjoyment of the play; they must take a more active part, and private theatricals became all the rage. During the whole of the eighteenth century down to the Revolution there was hardly a great house in town or in the country without its stage. The Duchesse du Maine had her own theatre at Sceaux, for which Voltaire wrote plays, and in which he acted himself. The Abbesse de Chelles, the daughter of the Regent, had one in her abbey; Madame de Pompadour acted at Versailles, and Madame de Rochefort at the residence of her father, the Duc de Brancas; the Duc d'Orleans, the Prince de Conti, the Comte de Clermont (the Abbé of St. Germains), Madame d'Epinay had each their own theatre; Marie Antoinette had one in every palace of the Crown. French people went mad with the craze. On the other hand, the philosophers, especially Rousseau and D'Alembert, protested against it, and the Church condemned it. Following up an old and cruel law, religious burial was refused to the members of the Comédie Française, whilst, with that inconsistency which is so often to be met with in the French eighteenth century, the actors of the Italian playhouse and singers and dancers were interred in consecrated ground. But in spite of philosophical and clerical opposition, the mania increased. Professionals took part in private theatricals, and became intimate with their patrons. Intrigues were the inevitable result. The charming Comtesse de Choiseul Stainville was made the scapegoat for all the fair offenders, and her jealous husband shut her up in a convent for the rest of her days. Unabashed by this warning, two great ladies who were enamoured of the same actor fought a duel for his sake, and one was seriously wounded. He might have thought himself the equal of the Duc de Richelieu. The conceit of the actors knew no bounds. Baron was playing cards with the Prince de Conti, and coolly offered him a wager of a hundred louis. 'Done! Britannicus,' answered the Prince smiling. He was acting one night, and spoke so inaudibly that some one in the audience cried out, 'Speak louder!' and he replied, 'Yes, and you speak lower.' But he knew the public, and being made apologise, he said, 'I never felt more than I do on this occasion the bitterness and lowness of my profession,' upon which he was vociferously cheered.

Baron,
1653-1729.

Lekain, the greatest tragedian of the century— of whom Louis XV. once said, 'He made me cry; I who never cry!'—was more modest. When he retired from the stage he was congratulated on having acquired both glory and money. 'As to the glory,' he said, 'I cannot boast of having acquired much; and as to the money, I have even less reason to be satisfied; you would not believe that my share of the earnings hardly amounted to 12,000 francs a year!' 'The deuce!' exclaimed an old officer, on hearing this. 'You, a vile stage-player, are not satisfied with 12,000 francs, while I, who sleep on a

Lekain,
1728-1778.

cannon and give my blood for my country, am happy to obtain a pension of a thousand!' 'Ah!' retorted Lekain, 'do you reckon at nothing the right you have to speak to me thus?'

Sophie Arnould, the singer, excelled in witty replies, which, like those of M. de Bièvre, have been collected and published. A lady more famed for her looks than her wit complained of being beset by a host of admirers. 'Oh!' said Sophie, 'it is easy for you to get rid of them. You need only talk.'

A critic of Beaumarchais' play, 'The Marriage of Figaro,' told her it would be a failure.

'Yes,' said she, 'so it will, but it will fail fifty times running.'

She one day met a physician with a gun on the look-out for game. 'Where are you going in this way?' she asked.

'To see a patient,' he answered.

'Oh! doctor,' she replied, 'you are evidently afraid of missing him.'

Her last words were addressed to her confessor, to whom she said, 'I am like Mary Magdalen—I shall be forgiven because I have much loved.'

With these words the curtain may be dropped on the reign of Louis XV. May it be judged as indulgently as Sophie Arnould judged herself.

Louis 16.

LOUIS XVI. AND MARIE ANTOINETTE

Louis XV. was fond of saying that he owed an account of his government to God alone, but when he lay dying of the smallpox he begged his successor to express to the Court the shame he felt for his scandalous conduct. According to custom, his body should have been embalmed, but the condition it was in repelled the physicians. 'Do your duty,' peremptorily ordered the great dignitary of the Court who had to preside at the operation. 'Yes, if you do yours,' they answered. It was the duty of that official to hold the King's head. But this he could not bring himself to do, so Louis XV. went uncared-for to his grave.

From the great rush in the passages of the palace towards their rooms, the new King and Queen knew that they had succeeded to the throne. Louis XVI., who was twenty years of age, and Marie Antoinette, who was nineteen, fell on their knees, and exclaimed, 'Protect and direct us, O God! we are too young to reign.'

Providence never sentenced two human beings

Louis XVI., 1754-1793.

to a sadder fate than in calling the grandson of Louis XV. and the daughter of Maria Theresa to the throne of France. That a sweeping change in the system of government, and that popular reforms on the broadest scale were imperative, that the old *régime* was doomed and must make way for a new order of things, that, in one word, a Revolution was imminent, was apparent to all save the most dull-witted. To avert a catastrophe at such a crisis a sovereign was needed of the highest capacity and the strongest will. Louis XVI. was a well-meaning, conscientious youth, who had been well and carefully educated, but of all the men in his kingdom he was perhaps the least fitted for the colossal responsibilities of the position to which he was called. He was entirely devoid of the most ordinary qualities of statesmanship, to say nothing of those which go to make a ruler of men. He could not see beyond the current requirements of the moment, and even with these he was unable to deal effectively as they arose. He was in the hands of his Ministers, but was incapable of appreciating the talents of those who were able to render efficient service to the State, and he accepted the offices of advisers who were forced upon him by Court intrigues, while he changed them with as much facility as he changed his coat. But the greatest of his defects was his fatal indecision and weakness of purpose. Louis XV. paraded his vices, but he never brooked any contradiction of his royal will, and he dazzled the minds of the public by the magnificent ceremonial of the Court functions. Louis XVI. had no vices, but he lowered the public respect for his person by the uncouthness of his manner, while the prestige of the Crown suffered by reason of the retrenchments he made in the pageantries of his predecessor.

Yet even a cleverer man than the King and a wiser woman than the Queen would have been deceived by the condition of France immediately after their accession. The heart of the masses went out to the young couple, and the greatest expectations were raised by the mere fact that a young king had succeeded an old one. The carrying out of some commercial and financial reforms gave a momentary appearance of prosperity to the country, and satisfied the immediate wants of the people. But the improvement was temporary. The feudal system, though it had long been bereft of its military character, still subsisted with all its vexatious privileges ; agriculture was more depressed than it had ever been, while underlying and undermining the whole fabric of the State was the financial rottenness which, though the people were only dimly acquainted with it, was the rock on which the State really foundered.

The King was an autocrat, but only an autocrat in name, as he was already passing under the control of public opinion. At the outset of his reign democracy was merely an intangible cloud, but it was steadily shaping itself into an ominous mass. The common people proclaimed their grievances ; the middle class were a powerful body whose demands could not be ignored ; the privileged orders closed in on the throne like an octopus, smothering its vitality in their grip. To satisfy any one section of his subjects was to antagonise the others. It is easy to be wise after the event, and now that over a century has passed since the Revolution, the critic may, according to his opinions or experience, map out the line of conduct that the King and Queen, the upper, middle, and lower classes should have followed, so as to achieve constitutional liberty without the violent uprooting of ancient institutions and the shedding of innocent blood which took place. He might say that if Louis XVI. had been a Henri IV. and Marie Antoinette a Blanche of Castille, or—without going so far for a parallel—a Maria Theresa, there would have been only an innocent little Revolution, without an emigration, a confiscation of property, the September massacres, the butcheries of Lyons, the guillotine, the ' noyades ' of Nantes, and the multitude of miseries that followed. A strong sovereign would have sent the discontented nobles to the Bastille and shot down the howling mobs, and granted reforms gradually but firmly ; every one would have been happy

Marie Antoinette.

and content, and all would have been for the best in the best of all possible worlds. But in criticising, nay, in condemning the conduct of the King, some allowance should be made for the racial idiosyncrasies of the French people, to which the Revolution owed its origin and character. Unquestionably, had Louis XVI. possessed even ordinary intelligence, the cataclysm might have been deferred or have been made to follow a different course. But it may be asked whether the condition of France and the temper of her people did not make the Revolution unavoidable at the time it occurred ; or, assuming that it could have been postponed, whether, whenever it came to pass, it would not have partaken of the character it did in 1789. The Revolution apparently brought to the people of France the realisation of their most ardent dreams and desires. Liberty, equality, and fraternity were not empty words but facts. Yet seven years after 1793 the French people submitted to the fiercest despotism they had ever known, after the fall of the empire they tried a constitutional monarchy, then another more limited monarchy, then another republic, and then again another empire. Finally, came the Commune. Every generation in France during the last century, in short, has witnessed a revolution.

When Louis XVI. was Dauphin he was asked by what name he would like to be known. ' I should like,' he replied, 'to be called Louis the Severe.' Had he been severe with his wife, his Ministers, his friends, and his people, he might have died in his bed. But he was mere dough in their hands, to be kneaded at their will. When at his coronation the crown was placed on his brow, he muttered feebly, 'How heavy it is!' Before many years had passed its weight had crushed him down. He should have been born to the position for which nature intended him —a huntsman, a mechanic, a bourgeois, or a farmer. He was shy, awkward, and ungainly; his coarse laugh and his gross appetite, which never deserted him under the most trying circumstances, made him appear ridiculous. Louis XIV. was a Jupiter, Louis XV. an Apollo; but Louis XVI. had no seat among the Olympian deities, unless, from his passion for the forge, he were styled a Vulcan. It may, at least, be said for him that he was honest, loyal, pious, and moral, and altogether one of the best-hearted men in his kingdom.

One day he was out hunting, and he met a peasant, of whom he inquired why the hay had not yet been made. 'Sire,' replied the rustic, 'the keepers have forbidden haymaking before the autumn, to save the partridges.' 'And I,' replied the King, 'I order you to make the hay at once if you wish it. It is not right that you should lose your profits to save my game.'

Shooting and hunting over the property of the tenants was the exclusive right of the landlords, for which they paid no rent or indemnity; a relic of feudal times that exasperated the rural classes, whose harvests were ruined by the game and the sportsmen. Count Dillon, Archbishop of Narbonne, was an example of many of his class who devoted their time to hunting, instead of to the care of the dioceses of which they had charge. 'You hunt so much yourself,' said Louis XVI. to him sternly, 'how can you prevent your curates from hunting too?' But the Bishop replied with the carelessness of the grand seigneur, 'Sire, were my curates to hunt it would be their own vice; for me to do so is the vice of my ancestors.' Louis XVI., unlike his family or the members of the Court, was economical without being parsimonious. Horse-racing had been introduced into France shortly after his accession, and at a race meeting the Comte d'Artois, his brother, who was himself plunging heavily, invited the King to have a bet; 'Yes,' said Louis, desirous of giving the Count a lesson, 'I will wager three francs on your horse.' He never participated in the gambling at which large sums were lost at Court, and which led to discreditable scenes at the palace. Strangers were admitted to these gaming parties whose only recommendation was that they would gamble for large stakes; and finally the arrangements grew so lax that card-sharpers and even pickpockets found their way into the palace.

The Queen, whom Louis tenderly loved, was inordinately fond of jewels in her youth, and the King, wishing to reprove her gently for this folly, said to her one day, as he was presenting her with a magnificent diamond aigrette, ' Pray wear this ornament, which you hardly require to set off your beauty. It will be all the more welcome to you as it does not increase my expenditure, for I have had the diamonds since I was Dauphin.'. It was customary for the daughters of the King to receive a set of diamond ornaments on the day they made their first communion, but Louis XVI. informed the Princess Royal that he intended to abolish this expensive practice. ' My daughter,' he said to her, ' you are far too sensible to value artificial adornments the day you should be engrossed with the desire of adorning your soul ; besides, while the distress of the people is so great, I feel sure you will gladly dispense with precious stones when you know that the poor have to do without bread.' He reduced the number of his household, with the result that he was laughed at by the people for his penny-wise economy, while the officials, whose salaries suffered by the reform, were affronted. One of these, the Duc de Coigny, insolently told the Queen that they were no safer in France than they would be in Turkey. The

King on another occasion took Count Dillon to task for being heavily in debt, but all the satisfaction he received was, 'Sire, I shall inquire of my steward, and shall have the honour of rendering an account to your Majesty.' As Louis Blanc says, speaking of the King's position in his 'Histoire de la Révolution,' 'He was estranged from the people by his weakness, and from the aristocracy by the purity of his life, and he stood alone, a stranger to the nation, a stranger in his own palace ; on his throne he was like a traveller lost on the summit of a mountain.'

The love of Louis XVI. for his people was not a phrase but a reality, and the first proof he gave of it was by abolishing the practice of torture. A lady once asked the Duc de Richelieu, 'What are the chief traits of the branches of the House of Bourbon ?' 'They each have a predominating taste,' replied the Duke ; 'the reigning house likes hunting best, the Orleans pictures, and the Condés war.' 'And Louis XVI. ?' further inquired the lady. 'His people,' rejoined the Duke. 'You and I are the only two men who love the people,' Louis XVI. told Turgot in the first years of his reign ; and in 1789, when the Deputies from Brittany, according to custom, knelt at his feet at an audience, he raised them up, saying, 'Rise, I am your father ; the place of my children is not at my feet.'

Turgot's appointment to the Controllership of the Finances had been proposed to the King by the then principal Minister, M. de Maurepas. ' But,' objected Louis XVI., who attached more importance to religious observances than to the possession of administrative capacity, ' I am told that M. Turgot never goes to mass.' ' Sire,' answered the old Minister, ' the Abbé Terray went daily.' The Controllership of the Abbé Terray, under Louis XV., had resulted in bankruptcy. Turgot, as is well known, was perhaps the only man in the kingdom who might have saved the monarchy ; but the inability of the King to appreciate his intelligence, and the cupidity of the courtiers, against which Turgot was proof, soon combined to drive him out of office. The reforms he effected were so drastic that they even staggered his friends, who told him that he was proceeding too rapidly. ' You forget,' he replied, ' that in my family we die at the age of fifty.' As a matter of fact he lived to be fifty-three.

From first to last Louis XVI. never realised the immediate gravity of his position. On the 15th July 1789 the Duc de la Rochefoucauld awakened him at dawn, to tell him that the Bastille had been taken. ' Why, it is a riot ! ' exclaimed the King. ' Sire, say a Revolution,' replied the Duke. Still, though the King often compared himself to Charles I. and saw the axe looming in the distance, he could not really believe that the people would lay their hands on their anointed sovereign, and he regarded the seething agitation in the country as nothing more than foam on the troubled waters. He was too irresolute to act on any impulse or decision of his own; he gave way when he should have been firm, and when he should have given way he waited till it was too late to be of any good. In many cases, however, his indecision arose from the kindness of his nature, for he would never consent to shed the blood of his subjects. He was out hunting near Versailles on the 5th October 1789 when he was told by a breathless messenger that a horde of fishwives had arrived at the palace from Paris, and were accompanied by an angry mob. Asked what his orders were, he answered, ' Orders against women! Why, you are jesting.'

From the day of their accession Louis XVI. and Marie Antoinette lived in a fool's paradise. When their misfortunes commenced, and during the last few years of their life, they had, it is true, the painful consolation of witnessing many proofs of devotion. The Swiss Guards were massacred on the 10th August in the defence of the Tuileries; Madame de Lamballe, who returned from Italy to be with the Queen in her distress, suffered a hideous death in the September massacres; the Duchesse de Tourzel, the governess of the royal children, and

Madame Campan, the Queen's reader, only left Marie Antoinette when the Temple closed its doors upon her. Many other similar instances of loyalty could be quoted, but, on the whole, it may be said that the King was deserted at the very beginning of the Revolution by his friends. The Comte d'Artois and the Prince de Condé left France at the first sound of alarm, heading that emigration which deprived the throne of its principal mainstay. Gamain, the locksmith whom Louis XVI. had employed for many years at Versailles and had treated like a fellow-workman, turned informer, betraying the safe where the King kept his private papers, which turned out to be of a most compromising character. A youth whom Marie Antoinette had reclaimed from poverty, and whom she had brought up, so to speak, on her lap, became one of her traducers. The young Duc d'Aguillon accompanied the rioters to Versailles disguised as a fishwife on the fatal 5th October. Scores of people, in short, high and low, who had fawned at the feet of their sovereign during his prosperity, turned against him in his adversity. But it is needless to dwell at greater length on this gloomy picture of treachery and ingratitude.

Among all the so-called friends of the monarchy who wished, or said they wished, to see it established on a constitutional basis, Lafayette was the foremost. Lafayette, it is true, was never a personal friend of the King and Queen. Whether he was a traitor, as Marie Antoinette believed, an enthusiast in the cause of liberty, or merely an ambitious, vainglorious, and short-sighted demagogue, is one of those psychological problems which history has not yet solved. After their return to Paris from the flight to Varennes in 1791, when the Royal Family were received by him at the gates of Paris at the head of the National Guard, he asked for the King's orders. 'It is for me to receive yours,' replied the King, 'being your prisoner.' 'I pity the King's fate,' replied Lafayette, 'but I never concealed from him that were he to sever himself from his people, I should remain with the people.' 'True,' answered the poor sovereign, 'and I have just recognised that the people are with you.' But were they? As soon as the monarchy had been abolished Lafayette had to fly the country. He should have remembered a conversation he had had with Frederick the Great, when he was received by that sovereign at Berlin in 1775. They were discussing the American War of Independence, and Lafayette said that there never would again be any nobility or royalty in America, continuing for some time talking in that strain of his political hopes. 'I knew,' replied the King, looking fixedly at him, 'a young man who, having visited a country where liberty, equality, and

Gilbert de Motier, Marquis de Lafayette, 1757-1834.

fraternity reigned, imagined he could establish
the same condition of things in his own land.
Do you know what happened to him?' 'No,
sire,' answered Lafayette. 'He was hanged,'
replied the King. Lafayette was not hanged by
Louis XVI., but was imprisoned for five years
in the fortress of Olmütz by the Emperor of
Germany.

During the Restoration, as a member of
the Chamber, he showed constant hostility
to the Bourbons, by whom in consequence he
was detested. 'This Marquis,' says his contemporary, General Thiébault, of him, 'thought
to be a French Washington, and having failed
in the effort he then vainly endeavoured to
gain the popularity of the mob as a means of
attaining power. The Duc de Choiseul, who
went to see Lafayette on his return from the
War of Independence, called him a mere
pantaloon. He was, in fact, a burlesque figure
who wished us to accept appearances for reality.
Yet, it is only fair to say that from the Revolution to the close of the Restoration, a time
when men changed their opinions and customs
as if they were changing their shirts, Lafayette
displayed the greatest tenacity in maintaining
a consistent attitude. M. Lafitte has characterised him exactly in the phrase, "He is like
a monument that is constantly promenading
in search of a pedestal."' After the Revolution
of 1830 Lafayette was once more appointed to

the command of the National Guard, and for a
time he supported the Government of Louis
Philippe, but during the last three years of his
life he went into opposition. He died in 1834.

However much Louis XVI. may be blamed
for his incapacity as a sovereign, his private
character is worthy of unstinted admiration.

He never knew fear. When, on the 10th
June 1792, the Tuileries were invaded by
a furious mob and his life was in imminent
peril, a soldier of the National Guard told him
not to be frightened. 'My friend,' he answered,
placing the man's hand on his breast, 'judge
whether my heart now beats faster than it usually does.' From the day he entered the
Temple a prisoner, on the 13th August 1792,
until he left it for the scaffold, on the 21st
January 1793, Louis XVI. bore himself with
the true kingly dignity and the saintliness
of a martyr. He read much, historical works
chiefly, gave lessons to his son, and kept up
the spirits of his wife, his sister, and his
daughter. After a few weeks he was transferred to one of the towers of the building,
being thus separated from his family, and
allowed to see them only at meals. On
one of these occasions Simon the cobbler, and
future 'tutor' of the Dauphin, witnessing the
tears of joy the Royal Family shed on meeting,
muttered : 'Verily I believe these confounded
women are making me cry!' But he soon

mastered his emotion and brutally said to the Queen, ' *You* did not cry when you murdered the people on the 10th of August!' 'The people,' calmly replied Marie Antoinette, 'are much deceived with regard to our feelings.' On 11th December Louis was ordered to appear at the bar of the Convention to hear his indictment read. At first he appeared reluctant to obey the summons, which was delivered to him by Santerre, Governor of the Prison and Commander of the National Guard, but on reflection said : 'This is another act of constraint, but I must yield.' The Secretary of the Commune read out the decree of the Convention, but on hearing the words, 'Louis Capet shall be brought to the Bar of the Convention,' the King interrupted him with the remark, 'Capet is not my name, it is that of one of my ancestors,' and then added, 'I should have wished that my son had been allowed to spend the two hours with me that I have been compelled to waste with you ; however, this treatment is only in keeping with what I have endured these four months. I will follow you, not in obedience to the Convention, but because my enemies have the power in their hands.' When he arrived at the Convention and stood unmoved, placidly surveying the assembly, the President addressing him, said, 'Louis, the French nation accuses you ; you will hear the terms of the indictment. Louis, sit down!' Louis firmly denied the guilt with which he was charged on every count, and at the end of the preliminary proceedings he requested to be allowed counsel to defend him at his trial. On his way back to the Temple he was assailed with cries of 'Death to the tyrant! Long live the nation!' At the Monastery of the Feuillants he was provided with supper, where a clerk, who noticed that he was too weary to finish his food, snatched away a crust of bread he was absently holding in his hand and threw it into the street. 'Oh,' exclaimed the King, 'it is wrong to throw away bread at a time when it is so scarce!' 'And how do you know that it is scarce?' asked Chaumette, the Attorney of the Convention. 'Because the piece I have just been eating tastes somewhat of earth,' answered the King. 'My grandmother always told me,' returned Chaumette, '"My boy, you must not waste a crumb of bread"—you could not say as much!' 'M. Chaumette,' replied Louis, 'it seems to me that your grandmother was à woman of much common sense.'

Chaumette, 1763-1794.

The King was now no longer allowed to communicate with any member of his family. 'It is very hard,' he complained; 'why, my son is not yet seven years old.' Target and Tronchet were appointed by the Convention to act as counsel for the King, and on Target's refusal Malesherbes came forward and, in a letter to the Convention, volunteered to defend him.

In the course of the letter he said, 'I was twice called to the Council by one who has been my master, when every one aspired to that office. I owe him the same duty now that this office is considered perilous by so many.' Louis embraced Malesherbes when the veteran magistrate came to consult him in prison. 'Your devotion,' he said, 'is all the more generous as you are exposing your own life without the hope of saving mine.' And later on, when M. de Séze joined Tronchet and Malesherbes, he told them, 'I am sure I shall perish ; yet let us set to work on my trial as if I must win it ; and I shall win it, because my memory will be left without a stain !' He prophesied truly. The trial, having lasted several days, ended after stormy discussions by the Convention voting his death. When Malesherbes brought the news to the King he found him leaning on a table, his head in his hand, absorbed in thought. 'I have been thinking during the last two hours,' said the King, 'whether throughout my reign I ever deserved the smallest reproach from my subjects, and I swear to you with all my heart, now that I am about to appear before my God, that I have never had any other wish than the happiness of the people !' Louis requested the Minister of Justice to grant him a respite for three days so that he might prepare himself for the fatal moment ; he also asked to see his family again, and to be assisted by a priest whom he should select. The two last requests only were acceded to, and Louis was informed that he would be executed on the following morning. After having seen the last of his family and having spent several hours in prayer with the Abbé Edgeworth, he slept peacefully, and was called at five by his faithful attendant Cléry, the only servant the Royal Family were allowed during their long im-·prisonment. The King gave Cléry all he could dispose of—a few trinkets, his snuff-box, and a lock of hair.[1] When Santerre was announced Louis asked, ' You come for me ? In one minute.' Having handed his will to a municipal officer, he asked for his hat, and then said in a firm voice, ' Let us go ! ' The King was driven to the Place de la Révolution with the Abbé Edgeworth and two gendarmes, who had orders to stab him at once if any attempt were made at rescue ; but the precautions which Santerre had taken would have precluded success had an attempt been thought of. Paris was like an armed camp. Guns had been placed at all the principal points, and battalions of soldiers lined the streets. Not a word was uttered during that long drive, which took over an hour, the King all the time reading the prayers for

---

[1] After the death of the King, Cléry emigrated to Russia. The snuff-box, which contains the portraits of all the members of the Royal Family, is now in the Museum of the Hermitage.

the dying.   Even on arriving at the foot of
the scaffold and on beholding the guillotine,
he composedly finished a psalm he had begun.
When the executioner opened the door of the
vehicle Louis said one more prayer, returned
his breviary to the Abbé, and requested the
gendarmes to see to the safety of his confessor.
The executioner attempted to lay hands on the
King, who pushed him back, divested himself
unaided of his coat and necktie, knelt at the
feet of the priest to receive his last blessing,
and then ascended the scaffold.   Again the
executioner proceeded to take hold of him.
'What do you mean to do?' he asked.   'To
bind you.'   'Bind me!   I shall never consent
to this—it is unnecessary, I am sure of myself.'
But at his confessor's request he submitted to
his hands being bound and his hair cut.   Then
he quickly stepped to the edge of the platform,
and essayed to make a speech to the crowd.
'Frenchmen,' he began, 'I am innocent.   I
forgive the authors of my death.   I pray
God that the blood which is going to be
shed may never fall back on France and you,
unhappy people!' . . .   Here Santerre ordered
the drums to be beaten, the executioner seized
the King, and a few moments afterwards his
head was held up to the crowd, who raised
a feeble cheer and silently dispersed.   'Son
of St. Louis, ascend to heaven!' the Abbé
Edgeworth is reported to have said when the

knife of the guillotine fell. These words, however, were probably invented by the 'République Français,' in the issue of which published on the evening of the execution they first appeared. The Abbé on being questioned as to their authenticity said he had no recollection of having uttered them, as being overcome by emotion he had almost lost consciousness at the time.

Generations of partisanship have manufactured a deep encrustation of lies round the memories of the illustrious dead, which, in many cases, modern research has successfully removed. In others, however, it has still to fight the old traditions which are rooted in the popular mind, and obstinately resist eradication. During her life Marie Antoinette was defamed by her enemies ; after her death she was exalted by her admirers, and for over a century both parties—democratic and royalist—have continued to defame and exalt her. The one could see in her only a giddy and frivolous woman, a flighty and extravagant wife, an unpatriotic foreigner ; to the other she appeared a vision of loveliness, a cruelly maligned consort, and a heroic martyr. To steer between these two views would be to steer a wrong course. Both descriptions must, to some extent, be maintained if justice is to be done, for there were two Marie Antoinettes. There was the Marie Antoinette of the early and palmy days, who

Marie Antoinette, 1755-1793.

M

would not listen to her mother's advice, who
flirted and gambled, went to public masked
balls, drove out in gilt sleighs when the people
were dying of famine, who played soubrette
parts in private theatricals, who fled from Court
functions to the boudoirs of her friends, and
wasted large sums on trifles when the Treasury
was encumbered with debt.   Then there was
the Marie Antoinette of later years, the devoted
mother and consort, who could have found
safety in flight, had she consented to leave her
family in the Temple, but who never flinched
from the post of duty, bore up with unparalleled
dignity against insult and misfortune, and did
her best according to her lights to save the
monarchy ; the magnificent victim of her own
courage, the noblest martyr of a fallen cause.
There was no transition between the two
periods, no indication of the coming change ;
the great Marie Antoinette rose like a phœnix
from the ashes of her former self. In her youth
a sophisticated and ill-natured society placed the
worst construction on her flirtations, but even
had these imputations not been proved slander-
ous by this time, it could safely be asserted that
her pride would have made her proof against
temptation.   Her intimacy with her friends,
which evoked so much animosity, was the
natural yearning of a fond heart for affection ;
the expenditure at Trianon, one of the chief
grievances of the people, was a mere drop in the

ocean of the Crown expenditure. But she never understood that a queen must submit to the thraldom of her high position, and could not indulge in the same freedom of action as a private individual. Being of foreign birth, she should not have interfered with politics, or if forced by circumstances to take part in the affairs of the realm, she should have shown the strictest impartiality. She excited the jealousy of the Court by inducing the King to appoint her favourites to the highest offices, and she offended a suspicious people by showing her sympathy with Austria. Her desire was to be loyal to France and to exercise her political influence in a manner beneficial to the interests of the country, but her uncompromising conservatism, her hatred of those aristocrats, like Mirabeau and Lafayette, who in her opinion were untrue to the King in espousing the democratic cause, made her interference in State affairs disastrous in its effects. Up to the last she held to the ancient belief that the welfare of the country was identified with the personal fortunes of the sovereign and the maintenance of the old *régime*. So, when the evil day came, she appealed to her imperial brothers for assistance and armed intervention, oblivious of the fact that to invoke a foreign invader was the greatest offence she could commit in the eyes of the nation. To sum up — Marie Antoinette was gifted and accomplished, but was not clever in the ordinary sense of the word; she was high-minded but injudicious; French in spirit because of her husband and son, and French in her ways, but German in appearance, disposition, and tastes.

Marie Antoinette was fifteen years of age when she set foot on French soil. A pavilion had been erected at Strasbourg for her reception, and was decorated with tapestries representing the tragic scenes from the story of Jason and Medea. 'What an omen!' she exclaimed on entering it. Shortly afterwards she was harangued by the State officials in German, but she interrupted them at once, saying, with great presence of mind and an indescribable charm of manner, 'Do not speak German. From to-day I only know French.' The old King was delighted on seeing the Dauphine, and despite the penury of the exchequer, ordered twenty million francs to be spent on the marriage festivities. There was a splendid display of fireworks in the Place Louis XV.—now the Place de la Concorde, sometime the Place de la Révolution and headquarters of the guillotine. The stands which had been erected for the public broke down in the crush, killing hundreds of sightseers, whose bodies were buried close by in the Madeleine cemetery, where Marie Antoinette herself was eventually interred. This was the second bad omen. Fate was against her even before she arrived at Versailles. Fate first came in the guise of the aunts of the Dauphin, the daughters of Louis XV., four bigoted and

crotchety old ladies, who spent most of their
time in their own apartments at the feet of their
confessor, the due observance of the prescribed
etiquette being their sole thought, and their chief
enjoyment a good cuisine. They looked with
no friendly eye on the arrival of a beautiful
young princess who might weaken their hold
on the King and disturb the equanimity of
their petty existence. When asked by their
equerry for their orders when he was starting to
meet the Dauphine at the frontier, they replied,
'We have no orders to give when an Austrian
princess has to be fetched.' These old ladies
constantly used that baneful expression 'the
Austrian' when speaking of Marie Antoinette,
and it soon spread from the Court through
the country, clinging to her to the very end.
Marie Antoinette, feeling inexperienced and
isolated in the Royal Palace, naturally looked
to her nearest relatives for advice and society.
Her husband, a mere youth, treated her coldly
at first, and for some years was only a husband
in name ; her aunts, though masking their bitterness under an outward show of cordiality, intrigued against and did their utmost to discredit
her. These aunts—'Mesdames,' as they were
called—never relented towards Marie Antoinette. Whenever they were told of any action
of the Queen's or any opinion she had expressed,
they invariably replied, 'We should be much
surprised if she had thought things out like our

father or brother,' or ' We are always discovering
that the Queen holds opinions contrary to the
welfare of the House of France.' When the
silk merchants of Lyons drew up a petition
accusing the Queen of ruining their trade by
the preference she showed for plain white gowns,
Mesdames gave their patronage to the petitioners,
forgetting that they had been the first to in-
veigh against the Queen's fondness for dress.

Marie Antoinette was on intimate and happy
terms with her youngest brother-in-law, the Comte
d'Artois, afterwards Charles X. Both were
young and fond of pleasure, but she was in-
veigled by the Prince into those heedless follies
for which later on she had to pay so dearly.
She soon became estranged from her elder
brother-in-law, the Comte de Provence, afterwards Louis XVIII., for his wife hated her with
the jealousy of a plain woman for a beautiful
one, and the rancour of a haughty princess of
inferior rank for her royal superior. That
hate never waned. The Queen once criticised
the conduct of the Comtesse de Provence's lady-
in-waiting, and she spitefully replied, ' You will
only be Queen of France, you will never be the
Queen of the French !'

At first the youth and grace of Marie
Antoinette captivated the people, and at her
State entry into Paris, the Duc de Brissac might
truly say, pointing to the enthusiastic crowd,
' Madame, see! here are two hundred thousand

lovers of yours.' But three years later, on the occasion of her second State visit to the city, she was so coldly received that she asked, 'What have I done to them?' She had done nothing but good to the people, having contributed largely to charitable objects from her private purse. On becoming Queen she declined the customary gift of money from the nation, known as the 'Queen's girdle.' But during these three years she had plunged recklessly into the dissipations of Court life, obstinately refusing to be guided by her tutors, wasting her time in consultations with dressmakers and milliners devising the most extravagant costumes. Her brother, the Emperor Joseph II., came on a visit to Paris at this time. One day he found Marie Antoinette engaged in arranging a lofty device of feathers and flowers on her head. 'Is not my hair beautifully done?' she asked. 'Yes,' he curtly replied. 'That is a very cold "yes." Does not this head-dress suit me?' 'Well, if you wish me to speak frankly,' he replied, 'I think it rather light to wear a crown.' During these three years her enemies had been steadily at work defaming her to the public. Who were these enemies? They were, in the first instance, the King's relations, as has already been explained; then Madame du Barry, whom she proudly shunned; and finally the whole of the old Court. Marie Antoinette declared at the very outset of her married life that she would not receive

women who were separated from their husbands;
and going a step farther, struck off the list of
her entertainments the names of the many ladies
who had been compromised in intrigues.   But
these ladies were all of the bluest blood in the
land, and with their families and friends they
revenged themselves by misrepresenting everything the Queen said or did.   Their principal
Louis ally was the Duc d'Orleans, the first prince
Philippe
Egalité, of the blood royal.   Louis XVI. always dis-
Duc
d'Orleans, liked the Duke, and predisposed the Queen
1747-1793. against him.   But the King's dislike, and his
refusal to promote the Duke to the high offices
he coveted, were attributed to the Queen's influence, and she had to suffer in consequence.
The Duke took no pains to conceal his feelings,
and when the Dauphin's birth was announced he
publicly declared, 'The Dauphin will never be
my king.'   Marie Antoinette bitterly resented
these words, and when the Duke came to Versailles, after having converted a portion of his
gardens, now the Palais Royal, into arcades and
shops, she sarcastically said to him, 'As you are
now going to have shops, I suppose we may
only hope to see you now on Sundays.'   The
Duke never forgot this taunt, and he put
himself at the head of the class who libelled
the Queen, the very class whom duty and
interest should have prompted to stand by the
throne.

Marie Antoinette, brought up amid the rustic

simplicity of Schoenbrunn, was suddenly launched on the deep and treacherous waters of the French Court, where the observance of a rigid etiquette was considered by the nobility one of their most cherished privileges, a tribute to their position, and a distinctive sign of their rank. She rebelled thoughtlessly against its odious irksomeness, and by infringing its rules offended the persons whom she would have been wise to conciliate. She delighted in irritating, by wilful disobedience of their instructions, the Comtesse de Noailles and the Comtesse de Marsan, her two principal ladies, who made this etiquette a means of tyrannising over her. They retaliated for the ridicule she cast upon them by turning their relatives against her. The Queen was undressing on a cold winter night, and the maid was handing her the 'chemise' when the lady-in-waiting came in, to whom, as being of superior rank, the garment had to be given over. She could not touch it, however, until she had removed her gloves, and as soon as this operation had been performed the Duchesse d'Orleans, a princess of the blood, turned up, and after her the Comtesse de Provence, who was of higher rank still, so that the chemise had to be handed from one to the other, while the Queen stood waiting and shivering. At last, unable to contain herself any longer, she exclaimed, 'It is odious! What a nuisance!' The importance attached to the observance of etiquette may also

be judged from an episode related by Madame
d'Oberkirch in her Memoirs.   It was considered
disrespectful on the part of any lady to allude
to the looks of a princess.   At an audience
with the Princess Royal, then a girl of ten, she
complimented her on her good looks.   'I am
glad to hear this from you,' coldly replied the
child, 'but I am surprised that you should say
it.'   Marie Antoinette had christened her chief
monitor, the Comtesse de Noailles, 'Madame
Etiquette.'   Once, riding a donkey in her
private grounds, she had a fall, and she cried out,
laughing, 'Go and fetch Madame de Noailles ;
she will tell us what etiquette prescribes for a
Queen of France when she falls off a donkey.' [1]

Marie Thérèse, Duchesse d'Angoulême, 1778-1851.

In the seclusion of the Trianon, in the midst
of her relatives and a few chosen friends, the
Queen threw off the burdens of royalty and
became an ordinary mortal.   But Queens of
France had come to be regarded almost as super-
natural beings.   Plainly clad and unattended,
Marie Antoinette often walked at night in her
grounds with her two sisters-in-law ;   innocent
nocturnal expeditions, which gave rise to the
most infamous slanders.   It would have been
well if the Queen had been content with her
Trianon, but she purchased St. Cloud from the
Duc d'Orleans, adding it to the many royal
palaces already possessed by the Crown.   The
people were exasperated by her indulgence in

[1] Madame 'Etiquette' was guillotined in 1794.

this costly luxury, and while marching along the road to visit its grounds, they cried out derisively, 'We are going to St. Cloud to see the fountains and the Austrian!' Louis XVI., wishing to gratify the Queen's taste for gardening and rural pleasures, presented her with the Trianon, saying, 'You like flowers—I have a bouquet to offer you.' The coldness he had at first shown her had gradually given way to the most tender feelings, and he grew to love his wife passionately. For centuries the people had been accustomed to see their kings devoted to mistresses, whom they had made responsible for the follies of their sovereigns. Now that they no longer had a king's mistress to accuse, they turned on the Queen, and visited her with the responsibility for the King's incompetence and for the political troubles of his reign.[1] Had Louis XVI. consistently acted on the advice of Marie Antoinette, there would at least have been some continuity in his policy, but by repudiating it almost as soon as it was given, he dragged her name needlessly before the public and left on her shoulders all the blame for his own errors and weakness.

She committed a grave mistake in recommending Calonne to the King as Controller of the Finances. His only title to this post consisted in his being in favour with the Queen's friends, who procured his appointment in the

Charles Alexander de Calonne, 1734-1802.

[1] See Rivarol's Memoirs.

hope of being able to take advantage of his well-known levity for their own profit, and of securing his connivance at the extortions they levied in the Queen's name. The day after Calonne took the prescribed oath of office he said to the King, 'Sire, I have debts just now to the extent of two hundred thousand francs. I wish to say so at once, and also that I am expecting much from your Majesty's kindness.' 'Here are your two hundred thousand francs,' replied the King, as he handed him over the sum in debentures. Calonne pocketed the debentures, but did not employ them to pay his debts. 'I should never have burdened myself,' he jauntily told his friends, 'with the finances of the State had not my own been in such a bad condition.' To the petitioners who crowded round the new Finance Minister, he gaily said, 'If it is possible, it is already done ; if it is impossible, it shall be done.' To please the Queen and the Polignacs, and all the rapacious wolves of the Court, Calonne did both what was possible and what was impossible. When he had to resign, he left for England, where, one day discussing the fate of two Ministers whom Louis XVI. had dismissed, he said, 'They are only two rascals the more out of office.' 'Pray be indulgent, M. de Calonne,' was the malicious retort, 'you are forgetting yourself.'

Marie Antoinette, as a matter of course, came in for her share of the unpopularity which

Calonne soon achieved. Her own unpopularity was growing daily, chiefly because of her foreign origin, but in some measure also owing to her partiality for a few intimate friends, which antagonised the rest of the Court and society. Her affection for these friends was of a kind unprecedented in France. It was the outcome of her sentimental German nature, which induced her to place implicit trust in her friends, and to expect from them in return a devotion equal to her own, forgetting that the Queen of France had only sycophants and the throne only courtiers. The Duc and Duchesse de Polignac, and the Marquis de Vaudreuil, whom the Queen had loaded with favours, requited her kindness with ingratitude and insolence. M. de Vaudreuil, with whom she often played billiards, once, being unable to make a good stroke, in a fit of temper smashed the Queen's cue—a work of art, chiselled in ivory and gold. Another time, on complaining to Madame de Polignac that she had met some guests at her rooms whom she did not deem fitting company, that lady pertly answered, ' It is not because your Majesty deigns to come to my salon that I should exclude my own friends from it.' Of the privileged few who enjoyed the Queen's intimacy, the Princesse de Lamballe *Marie* alone proved worthy of her choice. For some *Thérèse de* *Savoie-* time she had been neglected for Madame de *Carignan,* Polignac, but the Queen assured her of her *Princesse de* *Lamballe,* continued affection. ' Never believe that I *1748-1792.*

have ceased to like you — it is habit with which my heart cannot dispense.'

In 1784 the Emperor Joseph II. requested the mediation of Louis XVI. in a dispute with Holland concerning the navigation of the Scheldt. Meanwhile the King concluded a treaty with Holland, which the Comte de Ségur, as War Minister, announced to the Queen, apologetically adding, ' I regret having been obliged to give the King advice which ran counter to the Emperor's wishes'; but Marie Antoinette replied, ' I cannot forget that I am the Emperor's sister, but I shall always remember that I am Queen of France and mother of the Dauphin.' Yet the Queen never got credit from the public opinion of the country for any feeling of loyalty to her adopted land. By the terms of the Dutch treaty, Louis XVI. had taken over the payment of a portion of the indemnity in which Joseph II. was indebted to Holland, and the Queen was accused unjustly of having obtained this condition for the benefit of her brother.

Whatever illusions she might still have had with regard to the feelings of the people towards her were rudely dispelled in the year 1785. An adventuress named Madame de la Motte had made a dupe of the Cardinal de Rohan, in order to become possessed of a magnificent diamond necklace which had been offered by the jewellers to the Queen, but had been declined by her. She induced a woman named Oliva, who bore some resemblance to Marie Antoinette, to impersonate her, and at night, in the gardens of Versailles, the Cardinal handed the jewels over to Oliva, believing her to be the Queen, with whom he wished to ingratiate himself. When the fraud was discovered, the Cardinal, Madame de la Motte, and her accomplices were all brought to trial. Marie Antoinette, if she were well advised, would have hushed up this affair at any cost, but her pride and dignity would not permit her to suffer the least suspicion. Madame de la Motte was found guilty, but the Cardinal was acquitted, as the Court was intimidated by the growing strength of democratic feeling. The great houses of Rohan and Condé publicly went into mourning for the insult done to a member of the family, and the people firmly believed that the diamonds had been in reality purchased for the Queen. Henceforth Marie Antoinette became daily more hateful to the people. In 1787 her unpopularity had reached such a point that her portrait could not be shown at the annual exhibition of pictures in Paris. Now that it had become known that she was exercising her influence in politics, the revolutionary party, afraid of the effect of her determined counsels on the King, assailed and calumniated her in the most violent language in the press. Matters came to a climax on the 5th October 1789, when, exactly five months after the meeting of the States-General, the Paris mob marched to Versailles, howling imprecations against the Queen. 'I know,' said Marie Antoinette to her attendants, who, on hearing the clamour at the gates of Versailles, assured her of their devotion, 'I know that they have come for my head, but I learnt from my mother not to fear death, and I shall face it with firmness.' Her martyrdom was beginning; she was never to know another happy day. The danger grew greater every hour; the Queen had to fly to the King's rooms, where she was met by his Ministers. She comforted them and endeavoured to raise their spirits. 'I am not afraid of dying,' she said, 'but only wish that those who are vile enough to become murderers had the consciousness of their crime, and would proclaim who they are.' These words had hardly been uttered when rifle shots broke the window panes and struck the wall close by the Queen. M. de la Luzerne, one of the Ministers, wished to protect the Queen with his body, but she beckoned him away, and as he feigned not to see her, she said, 'I guessed your intention, and I thank you, but I will not allow you to remain here. It is not your place, it is mine.' Outside the roar was increasing. 'We wish to see the King! we wish to see the Queen!' and the little Dauphin, trembling with terror, clung to his mother and cried out,

Mamma, I am hungry!' Madame de Staël, who was an eye-witness of the scene, says that the Queen, on being told by Lafayette that she must make the venture and appear before the mob, hesitated for an instant, and an instant only, and she then firmly declared, 'Should it be to my execution I shall go,' and she went on to the balcony with her children.' ' No children ! ' screamed the mob, and the children having been sent back, she stood there alone. ' They want to oblige us,' said the Queen, returning to the room, addressing Madame Necker, 'the King and I, to go to Paris, with the heads of our guards on their pikes.' And so it was. To Paris went the Royal Family, as prisoners from the palace which their ancestor had dedicated ' to all the glories of France.' From Versailles the Royal Family were driven to the Hotel de Ville, a distance of twelve miles which it took seven hours to accomplish. There Bailly, Maire of Paris, addressed the crowd, and, wishing to quiet them, quoted the words Louis XVI. had used on a previous occasion—' It is always with pleasure and confidence that I see myself in my good town of Paris.' He forgot the word 'confidence,' so the Queen whispered to him, ' Repeat " with confidence." ' The Tuileries, where they were to take up their abode, had not been inhabited for upwards of a hundred years, and no preparations had been made for their reception. The Queen turned to her suite, and said apologetically, 'You know I did not expect to come here.' An official inquiry was instituted into the events of the 5th and 6th of October, and a commission of magistrates was deputed to receive the Queen's evidence. But the only reply she gave to their questions was, 'I shall never turn informer against the King's subjects. I have seen all, heard all, and forgotten all.'

During the four years she was still allowed to live, insult, indignity, and ill-treatment such as would have put savages to shame, were steadily dealt out to Marie Antoinette. But the Queen rose to every emergency, and never once did she fail either as a queen or as a woman. Her children were her only con-solation in her troubles. The Dauphin was a most attractive child, and the Queen loved him intensely. On the occasion of Marie Antoinette's birthday Louis XVI. told his son that he was to gather a nosegay in the garden and present it to his mother, with a little speech of his own composition. 'Dear papa,' replied the boy, 'I have a beautiful flower in my own little garden; it is an immortelle; I want nothing more. My nosegay and my speech are quite ready. When presenting them to mamma I shall say, "I wish mamma to be like my flower."' In the spring of 1790 an attack on the Tuileries was expected. The King, hearing some stray shots, hurried to the Queen's room.

*Louis
XVII.,
1785-1795.*

She was not there. He then went to the Dauphin's apartment, where he found the Queen holding the boy in her arms. 'I was looking for you,' said the King, 'and was very much alarmed.' 'Sire, I was at my post,' she answered, showing him her son.

One year later came the memorable flight to Varennes, and the ghastly return to Paris. In that one night the Queen's hair turned gray. 'Her misfortunes have bleached them,' she wrote under a portrait painted for her about that time as a present for the Princesse de Lamballe. Seeing that her mistress had so sadly altered as to be hardly recognisable, Mademoiselle de Buquoy, a lady of the Court, could not refrain from bursting into tears, but tried to conceal her emotion. 'Do not hide your tears,' replied Marie Antoinette,' you are much happier than I am. Mine have been flowing secretly for two years, and I am obliged to swallow them.' The Queen had still an occasional gleam of happiness. At the conclusion of the service in the Tuileries it was customary to sing 'Domine salvum fac Regem,' to which the members of the congregation, the few devoted followers that still remained, spontaneously added 'et Reginam.' But the end was hurrying on. One year later, on the 20th of June 1792, the Tuileries was invaded, and as had been the case three years previously at Versailles, the mob were bent on taking the Queen's life. Seeing the

King's sister, Madame Elisabeth, at a window, they howled, 'There is the Austrian. Down with the Austrian!' The Guards asked that the mistake should be pointed out to them, but Madame Elisabeth, who had refused to leave France, and stayed with her brother throughout his peril, said, 'No, leave them under the delusion and save the Queen.' Marie Antoinette was in the Council Chamber, standing in the embrasure of a window with her son and her ladies, separated from the crowd by a great table, in front of which three rows of National Guards had taken up their position, headed by the brewer Santerre, who was the chief promoter of the disturbance. 'You have been misinformed, Madame,' he told the Queen; 'the people do not want to do you any harm. There is not one of them, if you cared, who would not like you as much as they do this child,' and he pointed to the Dauphin; 'save France! your friends are deceiving you. I will prove it by being your shield.'[1]   And he urged the crowd to move away, calling out, 'Look at the Queen, look at the Dauphin!' A sansculotte insisted that the cap of liberty should be put on the child's head. The Queen acceded to the request, but the poor little boy was half suffocated by the heavy headgear, so that Santerre himself was moved to pity, and said, 'Take it off, it is too hot for him.' The admirable dignity which the Queen displayed saved her

[1] 'Plastron' was the word he used.

from being insulted, but there was one virago
present who poured forth the foulest abuse on
her. 'Have I done you any personal injury?'
quietly asked Marie Antoinette. 'None, but
it is you who have ruined the nation!' 'You
have been deceived; I have married the King
of France; I am the mother of the Dauphin;
I am a Frenchwoman. I can only be happy
or unhappy in France. I was happy so long
as France loved me!' 'Forgive me!' said the
woman hysterically, bursting into tears, 'I did
not know you; I now see how good you are!'
But Santerre, who probably already regretted
having shown any sympathy with the Royal
Family, called out, 'The woman is drunk!'
The fearful ordeal to which the Queen was
subjected lasted till past eight o'clock in the
evening; then at last the palace was cleared
of the hideous crowd and Marie Antoinette
was able to join her husband again. They fell
weeping into each other's arms. Some deputies
of the National Assembly were present at the
interview, and were deeply moved; even the
depute Merlin de Thionville cried, but he
quickly dried his eyes and exclaimed: 'Yes,
Madame, I weep, but I weep for the misfortunes
of a good father and a good mother,—I have
no tears for a King.'[1] There being some fear

---

[1] In the course of time Merlin's opinions underwent
a curious change, for almost the day after the Restoration in 1814, he sent in his formal allegiance to the
monarchy.

the next day that the palace might be again invaded, the Queen at once said, ' My place is with the King. Our sister should not be alone in guarding him.' And as the little Dauphin nervously asked, ' Mamma, is yesterday not yet over?' 'Unhappy child,' she replied, ' yesterday will never be over for us.'

Louis XVIII., 1755-1824.

The Comte de Provence had remained in Paris until the King's flight to Varennes. He was luckier than his brother, and succeeded in then making his escape. Some few months previously it was reported that he intended to join the emigration, which caused a threatening crowd to assemble round his palace. The Prince at once ordered the gates to be opened, but that only the women were to be admitted to his presence. One of them went up to him and said, ' We hear you wish to leave Paris, but we beg of you not to do so. If you have any fears, my companions will come and keep guard here.' 'Your offer is a gratifying proof of friendship,' he answered, ' but I have no fear, and shall not leave Paris, for I shall never part from the King.' But another woman said, ' How if the King leaves us? You will then stay, won't you?' The Prince was somewhat puzzled, as he did not care to commit himself, so, looking intently at his questioner, he said, ' For such a clever person as you are, I must say you ask very stupid questions.' The

women laughed, kissed the Prince, and withdrew.

On the 10th August Paris rose in arms,
the Tuileries was besieged, the King lost heart,
and, being incapable or undesirous of offering
resistance, he said, 'There is nothing more to
be done here; I insist on our being conducted
to the Assembly.' The Queen rebelled against
this weakness, and exclaimed, 'You shall first
order me to be nailed to the walls of the palace.'
Eventually, however, she gave way, and turning
to the deputation that had arrived from the
Assembly, she asked, 'Gentlemen, do you
answer for the safety of the King's person, and
of that of my son?'—for herself she had no
thought. 'Madame,' they replied, 'we promise
to die at your side.' 'We shall return,' said
the Queen, as she left, to her ladies, who stood
by weeping. The Royal Family were taken to
the Assembly at seven in the morning. There in
the sweltering heat they were huddled together
in a small room used by the reporters, and
until two o'clock the following morning they
were compelled to listen to the debate which
ended in decreeing that the King should be
temporarily suspended from his functions, that the
Assembly should be dissolved, and the Convention summoned. At last the deputies sent Louis
Capet, as he was now called, his wife, and
children to the Prison of the Temple. On the
way the Queen bowed to a respectable-looking

man in the crowd. 'You need not put on such gracious airs,' he shouted back, 'you will not require them much longer.' The Queen's garments had become disordered and her shoes were worn out. 'You would not have believed,' she said, smiling, to Madame Campan, 'that a Queen of France could be in want of shoes.'

It is needless to dwell on the sufferings of the Queen from the day she entered the Temple —the 13th of August 1792—until she was sent to the Conciergerie on the 2nd of August in the following year. Madame de Lamballe, Madame de Tourzel and her daughter were at once taken to prison ; the two latter afterwards escaping almost by a miracle from the September massacres. One of the officials took a sudden fancy to Mdlle. de Tourzel, and saved both her life and her mother's. Madame de Lamballe was murdered and her head was borne on a pike past the Temple. The Queen hearing the uproar went to the window, and fainted on seeing the ghastly procession. She was now soon separated from her husband, and not allowed to see him until the eve of her execution ; and her son was torn from her arms to be 'educated' by the cobbler Simon. On quitting the Temple for the Conciergerie her head struck the gate, and on being asked whether she was hurt, 'Oh no!' she replied, 'nothing can now harm me any more.' In the Conciergerie she was treated like a common malefactor. A

Monsieur de Rougeville once gained admission to the prison and told her that a plot was being organised to effect her escape. 'Does your courage fail you?' he asked. 'My courage never fails,' she answered. But the plot was soon detected. Having been kept two months and a half in prison, being subjected to every conceivable hardship and indignity, the Queen was brought before the bar of the Revolutionary Tribunal on the 15th of October. Every reply she gave to her inquisitors might be quoted, but one or two will suffice. 'You have taught Louis Capet that deep art of dissimulation by means of which he has so long deceived the good people of France,' they said. 'Yes, the people have been cruelly deceived, but neither by my husband nor by me!' Then being accused of wishing to ascend the throne over the dead bodies of the patriots, she said, 'I have never wished for anything but the happiness of France. If France is happy, I am happy.' On the following day a long indictment was read in her presence, and she was under examination for several hours, during which ordeal she never lost her presence of mind, her control over her feelings, or her dignity. Being accused of having wilfully demoralised the Dauphin, a child of eight, to retain her influence over him, and when making no answer to this foul charge, she was asked why she remained silent, she exclaimed, 'If I do not speak, it is because nature revolts against my replying when such a question is put to a mother.' Then turning to the public, 'I appeal to every mother who is present.'

From nine in the morning of one day until four in the morning of the next she was kept under the harrow, and then sentence of death was at last pronounced. She heard it without saying a word or showing any emotion. At seven the same morning the executioner appeared, accompanied by a priest. 'This is the moment to show your courage,' said the priest. 'Courage! I have long learnt to have courage; be sure I shall not lack it to-day.' On leaving the Conciergerie she was assailed in the street with loud cries and insults. 'Alas!' she said, 'my woes will soon end—yours are only beginning.' When mounting the steps of the scaffold she inadvertently trod on the foot of the executioner; he uttered an oath and she begged his pardon. On the platform she fell on her knees and prayed aloud. 'O Lord,' she prayed, 'enlighten and move those who do me to death!' Then she rushed to the guillotine.

We may condone the crimes of the Revolution for the benefits it brought to the French nation, but the execution of Marie Antoinette was a dastardly and profitless murder, which cannot be forgotten or pardoned. Her errors —culpable as they were—fade to nothingness

when we think of the persecutions by which
she atoned for them. By her death she won a
glory and reverence by which her memory might
not have been hallowed had her life been spared,
whilst her judges—if judges they can be called
—it is only possible to regard with contempt
and disgust.

THE REVOLUTION

The French monarchy, which had lasted seven centuries in an unbroken line of succession, now collapsed within three years. The Revolution may be said to have begun on the 5th of May 1789, the day on which the States-General met at Versailles. Louis XVI. only reluctantly summoned this body, and it had no sooner been constituted than the democratic party at once formulated the rights they demanded, rights which they secured after a brief struggle of three months. The States-General comprised the three orders, or estates of the realm : the nobility, the clergy, and the commons. The nobility and the clergy had 300 representatives each, while the commons had 600. Each order was to deliberate and record its vote separately, and as the clergy and the nobility were in accord on most questions, their combined vote constituted a majority over the plebeian third estate. The commons clamoured for the fusion of the three chambers in one, and meanwhile they proclaimed themselves a National Assembly, with sole power to control the finances and levy the taxes. Many of the rural clergy, however, shared the views of the commons, and they succeeded in obtaining a majority in the clerical chamber for the fusion of the three orders. As this fusion would ensure the domination of the democratic party, the King, in order to prevent it, decreed the suspension of the sittings of the States-General, so that on the 22nd of June the commons on arriving at the palace found the doors of their chamber closed and guarded by soldiers. They proceeded forthwith to the tennis-court, where they assembled and bound themselves on the spot by a solemn oath not to separate until they had framed a constitution. On the following day the King again convened the three orders, went in state to address them, and in a speech which might have been fitting enough in the mouth of Louis XIV., but which was unsuited to the altered circumstances of the time, he annulled the decrees of the commons, gave a renewed sanction to the right of the clergy to the tithes, reasserted the privileges of the nobility, and concluded by dismissing the three orders to their three separate chambers. The clergy and the nobility obediently withdrew, but the commons, preserving an ominous silence, obstinately kept their seats. The King sent his Master of the Ceremonies, the Marquis de Dreux-Brézé, to repeat his commands.

'Tell your King,' replied Mirabeau, the spokesman of the commons, 'that we are here by the will of the people, and shall only leave at the point of the bayonet.' Louis XVI., who was said to have acted on the Queen's advice in this attempt to maintain the autocratic powers of the Crown, soon followed the bent of his own pliant nature, gave way before the popular storm his action had raised, and three days after Mirabeau had uttered his famous defiance, assented to the fusion of the three orders. Thus the democracy had triumphed, and the old *régime* was doomed.

Gabriel Honoré Riquetti, Comte de Mirabeau, 1749-1791.

The Comte de Mirabeau, who was described by his father as a 'monster of ugliness and immorality,' led a profligate and chequered life until the eve of the Revolution, but gave early promise of the extraordinary genius and oratorical powers to which he owed his title of ' the French Demosthenes.' He was only seventeen years of age when his uncle said of him, ' He will become the greatest wag in the world or the greatest man in Europe ; he will be a general, an admiral, a minister, chancellor, or pope, or anything he chooses.' His father, who never cared for his son, procured his committal to prison on a *léttre de cachét*, and was enraged at his dissolute life. Mirabeau on being liberated served for a short time in the army, but he again found himself in trouble, and was twice subsequently imprisoned at the instance of his father.

During these periods of enforced leisure he wrote a number of political and historical essays, which were marked by great erudition, and a series of tales of the most erotic kind, which sold better than the essays. He was always needy, and in his need he was ready to barter away his honour for gold ; being, as his contemporary Rivarol said, ' capable of doing anything for money—even a good deed.' Towards the end of the year 1780 he sued for a separation from his wife, conducting his case in person. But though he lost it, his eloquence made a deep impression on the audience in court. For the next six years Mirabeau strove to push himself to the front by every available means. He visited Holland and England, and on his return was sent on a secret political mission to Berlin. All the time he wrote diligently, for he had to live by his pen, and in his pamphlets on political economy and financial questions he revealed great knowledge of the affairs of the day, as well as versatility of mind and intellectual vigour of a high order. He also addressed a volume of letters to Calonne, in which he recorded his impressions and satirised public men so severely that it created a scandal, and was burnt, by order of the Parlement of Paris, by the hangman.

The advent of the Revolution at last brought Mirabeau his long-sought opportunity of playing a distinguished part in the history of his country.   Until then he had only acquired an unenviable notoriety by a contemptible life, but now his boundless energy and his extraordinary gifts found a congenial field for their development.   He first appealed to the nobility of his native country of Provence to nominate him in their interest to the States-General.   But they would have nothing to say to the reprobate, so he sought the suffrages of the commons of Aix, who at once elected him to represent them.   In a pamphlet, written shortly before his election, he had said, 'Injustice will never wear out my patience.   I have been, I am, and always shall be the one person to advocate a constitution. Woe to the privileged classes! . . . Privileges will come to an end, but the people are eternal.'   His eloquence and his enthusiasm for reform soon made him the leader of the National Assembly and the idol of the masses. The day following the taking of the Bastille the Assembly heard with applause that the King was about to come and address it in person.   Mirabeau rose and said, 'In this hour of grief, mournful respect should be our greeting to the monarch; the silence of the people is the lesson of kings.'   Nevertheless, the King's speech was received with loud cheers, for it ended with the words, 'I am one with the nation.   I trust myself to you.'

Though he was led by his impetuous temperament into making violent attacks on the then

Government, the aim of Mirabeau was to frame a constitution with a limited monarchy and a free people, and to become himself the chief Minister of the Crown. But his measures were wrecked between the impracticable temper of the Assembly and the stubborn resistance of the Court party. His intimate friend, the Comte de la Mark, who was also a friend of the Queen, tried to win Mirabeau over to the Royalist side, but such an alliance was not easily made, for Marie Antoinette, who regarded Mirabeau in the same light as his father had done, and shrank from him as from a leper, said, 'We surely shall never be reduced to the painful extremity of applying to him for help.' On his side Mirabeau spoke of his sovereign and the Queen as '*those people* who failed to see the abyss they were digging out under their feet,' while in the Assembly he continually advocated the most liberal measures. However, in time, La Mark, much to Mirabeau's delight, effected a compromise between him and the Court. His debts were to be paid, and in return he was to speak in the Assembly in the interest of the King. He had a private interview with the Queen which cemented for a while the compact between the great tribune and the Royalist party. But it got abroad that Mirabeau was untrue to 'the people,' and to undermine his influence his rivals published a libel entitled 'The Great Treason of the Comte de Mira-

o

beau.' On being shown the paper, Mirabeau exclaimed, 'I know it all well enough. I shall be taken from the Assembly dead or victorious'; and, rising to the highest pitch of eloquence, he carried the Assembly with him, and left it in triumph. But the relations between Mirabeau and the Court party soon became strained, as its leaders, though in a way anxious for his assistance, were afraid that if he carried the day they would ultimately be ground under his heel. He was hurt by their suspicions, and said to the indefatigable peacemaker, La Mark, ' *Those people* either do not understand or foolishly despise me.' He once more veered round to the King, but his death-knell had sounded, and the apostle of the Revolution and the greatest orator of the country died on 2nd April 1791, his constitution worn out by the excesses of his early life.

Shortly before he expired Mirabeau, hearing the report of a gun, muttered, 'Is this meant for the funeral of Achilles already?' His death was regarded as a national loss. The Assembly decreed that all its members should follow the body to the Pantheon, where it was buried in state; the theatres were ordered to be closed; the whole city went into mourning. Had Mirabeau lived in more settled times he might have been a great statesman and a powerful Minister. His talents were prodigious and his conceptions lofty, and though corrupt and inordinately vain, his love for liberty and the welfare of the people was sincere.

The next eighteen months witnessed the rapid rise of the Revolution, the growing domination of the Jacobin Club, and the development of the insurrectionary spirit of the Commune.[1] The hopes of the genuine lovers of freedom, who by dreamy and impracticable methods endeavoured to construct an ideal constitution on the foundations of the old order, were extinguished by the fierce fanaticism of a new class of men, the born leaders of the turbulent masses. In appealing to foreign powers for assistance the King had signed his own death-warrant. France could not brook the rule of a sovereign who called for an invasion to regain his authority, and conspired with the traditional enemy to rebuild a shattered despotism by the aid of foreign arms. At first the policy of the Court was only suspected, but

[1] Paris during the Revolution was divided into forty-eight sections or parishes, whose so-called active citizens formed a committee. These active citizens, who had to be twenty-five years of age, and paid taxes on three days' work at least, elected the public functionaries for each section, and also a second body of electors, who in their turn elected the representatives of Paris in the National Assembly, the judges, and other minor officials. The Municipality consisted of a Maire, sixteen Directors, a Council of ninety-six members, an Attorney for the Commune, two Deputy-Attorneys, and some clerks, all of whom were elected by the members of the section by a most complicated system of voting.

the suspicion it created determined the Assembly to deprive the King of the prerogatives he had still been allowed to retain. After his flight to Varennes the people took the law into their own hands, and committed the outrages which compelled the Royal Family to leave the Tuileries and take refuge with the Assembly. That body was dissolved in August, and when on 2nd September the Convention met for the first time, the Abbé Grègoire, in an inflated but impassioned speech, proposed the abolition of the monarchy and the establishment of a Republic. 'Kings,' he said, 'are from a moral what monsters are from a physiological point of view. Courts are the workshops of crime and the seat of all corruption ; the history of kings is the martyrology of nations.' The whole Assembly rose to its feet and assented to his proposal by acclamation.[1] On the previous day General Dumouriez had defeated the invaders of France at the battle of Valmy. But Europe was coalescing and arming. Some few months later, after the execution of Louis XVI., the Dauphin was proclaimed king by the adherents of the monarchy, and though a prisoner and prostrated by sickness, he commanded their allegiance as if he were seated on the throne. Over two

---

[1] The Abbé Grègoire also obtained acknowledgment by the Convention of the civil and religious liberty of the Jews and the abolition of slavery.

hundred thousand Royalists had emigrated, but a considerable portion of the people had remained loyal to the ancient order, and in every department there were large numbers of persons preparing to fight for 'God and the King.' The western provinces raised the White Flag; Lyons, the most important city after Paris, refused to recognise the authority of the Convention, and Toulon was handed over to the British forces. The clergy had to take the oath to the new Constitution under penalty of death, for there were priests who refused to conform, and who, in hiding in every town and village, fanned the flame of rebellion by working on the consciences of the faithful. The State was bankrupt and the country was given over to anarchy. France had to be saved from the foreigner and the Republic from the Royalists. On the 1st of February 1793 war was declared against England, Holland, and Spain, and three hundred thousand enthusiastic Republicans marched across the frontier. Commissioners were delegated to watch over the Generals who were in command of the armies, and if they showed the slightest hesitation about obeying the orders given them, they were sent before the bar of the Convention to render an account of their conduct. And in every province Commissioners were also placed, with full powers to cope, by the most drastic measures, with the chaotic condition of the country. An army was sent to 'pacify' the western provinces. Lyons was captured, and its defenders were shot down in files of hundreds at a time. Toulon was taken, and the rebels were put to death. At Nantes fifteen thousand persons were either shot or drowned in the Loire, and all the great cities following the example that had been set by Paris erected the guillotine *en permanence*.

The Convention was at first divided into two groups—the Girondists and The Mountain. The Girondists, who, though ardent Republicans, held moderate views compared to the members of The Mountain, had the democratic element in the provinces at their backs; while The Mountain was supported by Paris, the Commune, and the Jacobin Club. In all great national crises, especially in times of national peril, the boldest and most unscrupulous men carry the day. These were perilous times for the Republic and the men who wished to be at the head of affairs, for in fighting for power they were fighting for their lives. The Mountain, with Robespierre as their leader, were as sincere as the Girondists in their desire to consolidate the Republic on a firm basis, but they also desired supreme power, and were determined to give a short shrift to those who stood in their path. The Mountain had a majority, and they used it to destroy their rivals. On the 1st of May 1793 the Girondists were arrested and imprisoned for five months, and on the 1st of October, after a trial of five days, were sent to a doom they hardly deserved. With them perished Madame Roland, the young, attractive, and talented wife of a former Girondist Minister who had escaped, and who committed suicide on learning his wife's fate. When she was taken to prison, Madame Roland—who had always spoken and written in favour of a Republic, and was personally hostile to Marie Antoinette—was examined by the public accuser, and was told to cut short her answers. ' I pity you,' she replied ; ' you fancy you have laid hands on a great culprit ; you are anxious to prove me guilty ; how unhappy you must be at having such prejudices. You may send me to the guillotine, but you cannot deprive me of the satisfaction of feeling that I have a clear conscience and the certainty of knowing that posterity will avenge both Roland and me by branding our persecutors with infamy.' She was allowed counsel, and having chosen one, she said, ' In return for all the malice you bear me I wish that you may feel the same peace of mind I do, whatever its penalty may be.' On being condemned to death she declared, ' You consider me worthy of sharing the fate of the illustrious men you have murdered, and I shall endeavour to show the same courage on the scaffold as they have done.' On passing

Marie Jeanne Philipon Madame Roland, 1754-1793.

a statue that had been erected to 'Liberty' on the way to the guillotine, she uttered the well-known words, 'O Liberty! Liberty! what crimes are committed in thy name!'

From the day the Girondists fell, whoever displayed any moderation, whoever was suspected of lukewarmness towards the Republic, whoever was not an extravagant and fanatical patriot was arrested, and almost invariably put to death. The Government meant to rule by fear, and they instituted the Reign of Terror. There is no trustworthy record of the number who perished during that terrible time in the fights and massacres which took place throughout the country or on the scaffold, but in Paris an account was kept of the victims of the guillotine, and there alone, during the six weeks the Terror was at its height, thirteen hundred persons fell under its knife.[1] The ordinary jails of Paris being too small to lodge all the persons who were arrested daily, the principal mansions of the nobles were converted into prisons and filled with men, women, and youths, of all classes and ranks, who, having been detained there, some for many months, others only for a few days, were transferred in batches of twenty, thirty, or sixty to the Conciergerie, brought out the following morning before the Revolutionary Tribunal, asked a few stereotyped questions, and then hurried off to execution.

[1] According to other accounts the number was 2500.

A boy of fifteen was guillotined for having flung a rotten herring, which constituted his dinner, in the face of his jailer. A son was executed by mistake instead of his father. A lady named Mallet was tried and condemned in mistake for another lady named Maillé. The error was discovered before she was sent to the guillotine, but she was told, 'It is true you should not have been tried, but it does not signify, to-day will do as well as to-morrow for you.' A boy named Mellet was arraigned before the Tribunal instead of a man named Bellay, who was eighty years of age. The boy was asked his age, and he answered that he was sixteen— 'Well, you are eighty for the purposes of this charge,' calmly declared the judge, as he ordered him to be sent to the scaffold. Persecution produces martyrdom, and martyrdom produces heroism. The victims of the Reign of Terror, which lasted until the 27th of July 1794, were not all martyrs, for some were bloodthirsty and inhuman scoundrels who but too well merited the guillotine, but with few exceptions they all behaved like heroes.

By far the most wantonly savage of the Republican Commissioners was Lebon, who exercised the powers of a pro-Consul at Arras. The Marquis de Vielfort was lying bound under the knife of the guillotine, when Lebon, who was looking on from the balcony of a neighbouring house, made a sign to suspend

Joseph Lebon, 1765-1795.

the execution.   The mob, fancying he meant to pardon the condemned man, were greatly surprised at such unwonted clemency on his part. Lebon, however, took a newspaper from his pocket, read out a long account of a victory the Republican army had just gained, and ended by shouting to the Marquis, 'Villain, go and inform your friends of the news of our victories!' The execution, which had been suspended for twenty minutes, then followed its course.   One day Lebon had seven persons guillotined, all of whom were over eighty years of age, and he congratulated himself on the achievement by saying, 'We have done good work to-day; we have disposed of some old women.   What good were they?   They were useless on earth.'   As a rule while the executions—which Lebon always witnessed from his balcony—were proceeding, a band played an accompaniment to the revolutionary songs shouted by the mob.   Colonel Vaujour, one of the many inhabitants of Arras whom Lebon had sentenced to death, on being told of his fate, gaily asked, 'At what hour will the ceremony take place?'   'At two,' was the reply.   'All the worse,' he rejoined, 'two is my dinner hour; but never mind, I shall only have to dine a little earlier.'   He at once ordered a number of choice dishes and wines, and was still indulging in his meal when the fatal hour struck.   'I should have been glad of another morsel or two,' he said, 'but it does not signify ; let us go.' A dentist who was to suffer on the same day as Colonel Vaujour called out when he heard he had been sentenced to death, ' To the devil with the Republic! Long live the King ! ' He repeated those words on the scaffold, and then, turning to the executioner, he said, ' Come on and guillotine me.' When, after the fall of Robespierre, the promoters of the Reign of Terror met their deserts, Lebon, who was only thirty years of age, in his turn was sent to the guillotine. He wrote pathetic letters to his family, dined as usual, drank copious draughts of brandy, but on his way to the scaffold he faltered.

On the 6th of April the Convention decreed that every member of the Bourbon family should be arrested and held as hostages for the Republic, and on the following day the Duke of Orleans was sent to prison. It availed him nothing that he had called himself ' Egalité,' had become a member of the Convention, had voted for the King's death, and professed the most advanced Republican principles. No one can traduce his own order and be untrue to his name with impunity. He was dining at the Palais Royal with his friend Monville when Merlin de Douai, a member of the Convention, brought him the news of his arrest. ' Good heavens ! is it possible?' he exclaimed. Monville, who was squeezing the juice of a lemon over a fried sole, shrugged his shoulders—' What do you expect? ' he asked ;

'they have had all they wanted from your Highness; they have treated you as I do this lemon.' The Duke was sent to Marseilles for some months, was then brought back to Paris, where he was tried with the Girondists—being accused of having plotted to obtain the crown, and conspiring with General Dumouriez who had gone over to the enemy—and was condemned to death. He was conveyed to execution in a cart with four other men, one of whom, a locksmith named Labrousse, pointed at him with loathing and exclaimed, 'I have been condemned to death, but not to go to execution with this infamous wretch.' The Duke, though hooted and insulted by the mob, maintained the most placid composure, merely observing, 'Once they cheered me!' The executioner wished to take off his boots, but the Duke said, 'Leave them on; it will be easier for you to unboot the corpse.'

Thomas Mahy, Marquis de Favras, 1744-1790.

In 1790, shortly after Louis XVI. and his family had been conveyed to Versailles, and before the guillotine had been invented, the Marquis de Favras was accused by the Assembly of plotting to murder Lafayette and Necker, carry off the King, place him at the head of the army, and march on Paris. Favras was tried and sentenced to be hanged. Having read his own death-warrant at the request of his accusers, he quietly remarked, 'Permit me to point out that you have made three mistakes in spelling.'

A few days after the execution of the
Girondists, Bailly was also guillotined. He was
distinguished as an astronomer and scholar, and
was a member both of the Academy of Science
and of the French Academy. When the
Revolution broke out he gave up science for
politics, and entered the Assembly, over which
he presided in 1789, in which year he was
also appointed Maire of Paris. But on the 9th
July, being obliged to send troops against rioters
in the Champ de Mars who were clamouring
for the deposition of the King, he resigned
his office, left Paris, and went into hiding at
Melun. There, two years later, he was discovered by spies, brought before the Revolutionary Tribunal, accused of having secretly
corresponded with the Queen, and of having
fired on the people when putting down the riot
in the Champ de Mars. He was sentenced to
death, and being asked whether he wished to
appeal against the sentence, he replied, ' I have
always done what I could to ensure that the law
should take its course, and I shall submit to it
now, as you are considered its representatives.'
By a refinement of cruelty the scaffold was
erected in the Champ de Mars, the scene of
Bailly's supposed treachery to the people.
On 11th November 1793 the old man was
compelled to walk there from the prison on a
bleak, wet morning, and he arrived shivering
with cold and fatigue. ' You are trembling,'

*Jean
Silvain
Bailly,
1736-1793.*

shouted one of the crowd to him ; but Bailly answered, ' Yes, my friend, but it is only with cold.'

Of the great men of letters and philosophers of the eighteenth century, Condorcet alone survived to witness the outbreak of the Revolution. Astronomy, philosophy, political economy, and literature engrossed the labours of this versatile writer, the friend of Voltaire, D'Alembert, and Turgot, perpetual Secretary to and member of the Academy, contributor to the ' Encyclopædia,' and author of many works which were widely read at the time. Condorcet, who, like Bailly, was seized with the political fever of the day, was elected by the town of Paris to be one of its representatives in the Assembly, and afterwards sate in the Convention, where he was an ardent but moderate democrat. On 19th January 1793, during the trial of Louis XVI., Condorcet proposed the abolition of capital punishment, and that the King should suffer the greatest penalty, short of death. By this he was believed to imply that the King should be sent to the galleys, and his name was at once struck off the rolls of the Academies of Berlin and St. Petersburg by the King of Prussia and the Empress Catherine II. Condorcet, nothing daunted, did his utmost to obtain the King's reprieve, and during the succeeding few months he endeavoured to act as peacemaker between the Girondists and The Mountain.

Marie Jean Antoine Nicholas, Marquis de Condorcet, 1743-1794.

To the former he said, 'It would be better to try to check The Mountain than to quarrel with them'; and to the latter, 'Think less of yourselves and more of the commonweal.' The fall of the Girondists was Condorcet's death-warrant, and on 8th July 1793 he was ordered to be brought to the bar of the Convention. His friends had anticipated this terrible summons. They went to Madame Vernet, a relative of the famous painter, who kept a lodging-house for students, and appealed to her to save a persecuted man. 'Is he honest and virtuous?' was the answering inquiry, to which Condorcet's friends replied in the affirmative. 'Then let him come,' said Madame Vernet. 'Shall we tell you his name?' asked they. 'You can tell it me later on; do not lose a minute; while we are conversing perhaps he may be arrested.' This admirable woman behaved like a true heroine during the eight months she afforded the shelter of her roof to Condorcet. As he had been outlawed by the Convention the penalty for concealing him was death, but Madame Vernet never for a moment wavered in her determination to risk her own life in order to save his. It happened that a member of the Convention named Marcos came to stay at her house, and one day as Condorcet was leaving his garret to dine with Madame Vernet, the two men met on the stairs. Marcos stared hard at Condorcet, but passed on without

uttering a word. Madame Vernet, on hearing
of the meeting, rushed to his room and said to
Marcos, 'You have just met one of your colleagues whom the Convention has outlawed, and
whom I am concealing at the peril of my life.
Will you show less courage and generosity than
a woman?' Marcos made no reply, but thenceforward when he left the house he rarely
returned without a parcel of books for Condorcet. Meanwhile the Reign of Terror was
progressing, and Condorcet resolved not to
expose his landlady to any further danger for
his sake. 'Your kindness,' he told her, 'is
indelibly engraved on my heart, but the more
I admire your courage, the more I feel it to
be my duty as an honest man not to abuse it.
The law is clear. Were I discovered in your
house you would suffer the same penalty as I
should. I am outlawed. I cannot remain
here.' 'The Convention,' she nobly answered,
'has the power to outlaw you, but it has
not the power to remove you beyond the pale
of humanity. You shall remain.' Condorcet,
however, could not be persuaded to change his
mind, and on the 5th of April 1794 he left his
abode in disguise. On hearing of his flight,
Madame Vernet fainted. Condorcet wandered
all day in the streets, and spent the night in a
quarry close to one of the gates of the city.
For the next twenty-four hours he roved
through the woods of Clamart; then having in-

jured his leg, and as he was suffering the pangs
of hunger, he entered a small inn, and asked
for an omelette. 'How many eggs do you
want in it?' asked the innkeeper. 'A dozen,'
replied Condorcet, to whom the mysteries of
the differential calculus were more familiar than
the constituents of an omelette. The innkeeper
became suspicious on hearing this common work-
man ask for a dozen eggs for a single meal, and
he called upon Condorcet to show his papers.
The latter replied that he had none, and in
answer to a further question said he was a
carpenter. 'You a carpenter with such white
hands, and such fine linen in your shirt!'
incredulously exclaimed the innkeeper, whose
suspicions were now thoroughly aroused. Condorcet was searched and a volume of Horace
was found in his pocket. The police were sent
for, and he was marched off to prison, but on
the following morning he was found dead on
the floor of his cell, although whether his
death was due to poison or to natural causes is
still a matter of controversy. Such was the
pathetic end of this brilliant and accomplished
man, whom D'Alembert described as 'a volcano
covered with snow,' meaning that he concealed
a passionate nature under an appearance of outward coldness. Others, it is true, mockingly
called him 'an enraged sheep,' because of his
seemingly weak disposition ; but Voltaire, when
Cordorcet was delivering a disquisition on 'an

P

honest man,' said of him, 'They are honest men at whose head you are.'

Mme. de Condorcet, 1765-1822. Condorcet had married Mademoiselle de Grouchy, the sister of the future Marshal of that name, a beautiful woman and a talented writer. When her husband was hiding under Madame Vernet's roof, she visited him daily to solace him with her conversation, and as a means of diverting his mind from his distressing position she made him write an essay on 'The Progress of Human Thought.' After her husband's death she was imprisoned, but was saved from the guillotine by the fall of Robespierre. Napoleon, on meeting her one day, gruffly said, 'I don't like women who meddle in politics.' 'You are right, General,' she replied, 'but in a country where their heads are cut off it is only natural that they should like to know why.'

There was no more conspicuous figure among the chief actors in the drama of the *Georges Jacques Danton, 1759-1794.* Revolution than Danton. The most eloquent orator after Mirabeau, and the most influential member of the Convention next to Robespierre, his athletic figure, his terrific countenance, his magnificent voice and rhetoric appealed to the imagination of his contemporaries, and he appeals even now to our sympathy because of his tremendous energy and great talents. A master of phrases and with unrivalled powers of speech, he was great not only as a popular tribune, but as

an organiser. When in 1792 the Duke of Brunswick was leading the Allied Forces against France,
the Government lost their head, they even talked
of flying and leaving Paris to its fate. Danton
quieted the people, sent Commissioners into the
provinces to arouse the cities to a consciousness
of the national danger, proposed that domiciliary
visits should be made in Paris to seize the
Royalist conspirators and secure the arms they
had secreted, and restored confidence by recommending the most stubborn resistance to
the invader. Again on 2nd September, when
it was reported that Verdun had fallen, and
Paris was in consequence stricken with panic,
Danton appeared before the Assembly and made
an impassioned speech, ending with the famous
exhortation, ' The tocsin which is going to
sound is not a sign of alarm ; it is meant to
herald the onset on the enemies of the country ;
to drive them back we only require audacity,
more audacity, and always audacity.'

From the outset of the Revolution Danton
belonged to the most advanced party, advocated
the most extreme measures, and shared the
responsibilities of the Reign of Terror. Yet it
is wellnigh impossible to determine the precise
extent of his personal part in the outrages and
the wholesale shedding of blood which were the
outcome of the policy with which he was
associated. There may be no direct proof of
his having arranged the attack on the Tuileries

on the 10th of August, or the massacres in the prisons on the 3rd of September, but all the evidence we now possess tends to show that if he did not instigate the massacres he gave them his support and approval.   Nor can it be over-looked that they were planned and carried out by the Paris Municipality at a time when he was a member of that body, and could scarcely have failed to be cognisant of what was being done, or that he consented to become Minister of Justice on the very day after the massacres took place.   Danton, in fact, hesitated at no measure which in his opinion was calculated to further the revolutionary cause, yet though he goaded on the people to the perpetration of these excesses, unlike his colleagues he saved many lives by his personal intervention.   He voted for the death of the King, assisted in the crea-tion of the Revolutionary Tribunal, and sided with The Mountain.   But here again he rescued many people from the guillotine, and only con-sented to the impeachment of the Girondists after having long and fruitlessly attempted to reconcile the rival parties. ' I called on Danton, who was ill,' relates Garat in his Memoirs, ' and saw at once that his indisposition was merely caused by the grief and dismay he felt at the turn of events.   " I shall be unable to save the Girondists," were his first words, and heavy tears rolled down a face whose features might have been those of a Tartar.'   Danton was walking in his garden in the country, when a friend rushed up to him, holding a paper and calling out, 'Good news! good news!' 'What news?' he asked. 'The Girondists have been condemned and executed,' was the reply. 'And you call this good news, you wretch!' answered Danton as his eyes filled with tears. 'The death of the Girondists good news!' he repeated. 'Unquestionably; were they not factious?' 'Factious!' rejoined Danton, 'are we not all factious? We all deserve death as well as the Girondists, and we shall have to share the same fate.'

Though he supported Robespierre and the policy of the Reign of Terror, Danton provoked the hatred of the more violent Terrorists by his comparative moderation. For some time his friends foresaw the inevitable end, and advised him to strike down Robespierre before he was struck down himself. But having grown indifferent to danger, or weary of the horrors he had witnessed, he replied, 'I prefer being guillotined to guillotining others,' and when his friends besought him to seek safety in flight, he proudly retorted, 'They will not dare to touch me, I am the key of the structure.' They continued to press this counsel upon him, and he answered, 'I should leave my country behind me; I cannot carry it away on the soles of my boots.' On the 31st March 1794 Danton was arrested, with fourteen other members of the Convention. On his way to prison he mournfully said, 'On this very date I established the Revolutionary Tribunal. I pray pardon of God and the people. It was intended to prevent another 3rd September, and not to become the scourge of humanity.' Being asked his name and place of abode at the bar of the Tribunal, he answered, 'My abode will soon be in nothingness, and my name will live in the Pantheon of history.' When the condemned men arrived at the foot of the guillotine on 15th April, one of their number, Herault de Sèchelles, asked to be allowed to give Danton a last embrace, but the request was refused. 'Fool!' said Danton to the executioner, 'you cannot prevent our heads from meeting in your basket.' When his turn came he said, 'You will show my head to the people; it is well worth the trouble."

Antoine Lavoisier, 1743-1794. On 8th May 1794, three weeks after the death of Danton, Lavoisier was executed in company with twenty-seven other ex-Fermiers-Generaux. By putting to death this illustrious scholar and blameless man, who may be considered the founder of modern science, the Revolutionary Tribunal reached the climax of infamy. But he instituted the *octroi*—the toll-houses placed at the gates of Paris—a measure by which he incurred unpopularity, and moreover, he had been a Fermier-General, which was

alone sufficient to ensure his doom. On hearing
that his former colleagues had been arrested he
voluntarily gave himself up, but he begged the
Tribunal to grant a respite of a few days to con-
clude some experiments on which he was engaged.
'The Republic is in no need of scholars,' was
the brutal reply, and both Lavoisier and his
wife were carted off to the guillotine.

On the 9th of May Madame Elisabeth was
removed from the Temple to the Conciergerie.
'Do not cry,' she said to her niece, the Princess
Royal, when the municipal officer came for her;
'I shall return.' 'No, you will not return,'
brutally interposed the official; 'put on your
cap and come!' 'What is your name?' she was
asked the following day, when she appeared
before the Tribunal. 'Elisabeth of France,' she
replied. 'Where were you on the 10th of
August?' was the next question. 'At the side
of the King, my brother, in the Palace of the
Tuileries,' she answered. 'At the side of the
tyrant, your brother!' rejoined the judge.
'Had my brother been a tyrant,' she proudly
exclaimed, 'neither you nor I should be where
we are now! Why put all these questions?
You simply desire my death! I have offered
my life up to God, and shall be happy to meet
in heaven those I so dearly loved on earth.'
Madame Elisabeth was conveyed to execution
with twenty-five other condemned prisoners,
whom she exhorted to die with piety and

fortitude, and without that display of cynical bravado which some of the condemned occasionally affected on the guillotine. The Princess was kept waiting at the foot of the scaffold until the last of her companions had been executed. As their names were called the ladies kissed her, while the men bowed deferentially as they passed in front of her to their doom. When her own turn finally came, the executioner, in seizing hold of her hand, tore off the shawl she was wearing, exposing her neck and shoulders. 'In the name of your mother, sir,' she cried out, ' cover me up!' and the executioner acceded to her entreaty. Thus perished a princess whose whole life had been spent in the most sublime devotion to God and her family.

Guillaume Lamoignon de Malesherbes, 1721-1794.

The government of the Republic was carried on by various committees, whose members were chosen from the Convention. During the Reign of Terror the Committee of Public Safety, which was then composed of Robespierre, St. Just, Couthon, Collot, Billaud, and Barère, concentrated the whole authority of the State in its hands. To their disgrace they allowed a man to be condemned whose services to the country in the past, and whose courage on a most critical occasion should have especially recommended him to their mercy. Malesherbes was a member of an old and distinguished legal family. When his father was appointed Chancellor of the Paris Parlement he succeeded him, at the age of thirty-four, as President of the Cour des Aides, in which position he firmly set his face against the financial abuses of the Court. In 1758 the Prince de Conti was deputed by Louis XV. to rebuke the Cour des Aides for its refusal to accede to the King's repeated demands for money. 'Prince,' replied Malesherbes, 'it must be very dreadful to hear the truth, as so many obstacles are thrown in its way, and it is so vigorously resisted by the throne.' Undaunted by the rebuke from the King, Malesherbes continued to address remonstrances to him, which Louis XV. disregarded, and went on levying fresh taxes and infringing the liberties of the Parlement. Malesherbes, in virtue of his office, acted as censor of the press, and he earned much popularity by his toleration in sanctioning the publication of the 'Encyclopædia' and of many other works written in the liberal and democratic spirit of the day. The Encyclopædists were assailed on all sides as being the foes of law and religion, and were accused of poisoning the minds of the people. Malesherbes received an order from the Government to seize Diderot's papers, but took care to send him word an hour beforehand to enable him to secrete them. 'Say I have no time,' answered the philosopher. 'Where am I to hide them?' 'Let him send them to me,' replied Malesherbes on receiving the message, 'they will then be safe.' Meanwhile his father had been banished for his attempts to protect the members of the Parlement from the oppression of the Crown, and the Chancellorship had been given to Maupeou, who recommended that the penalty of death should be decreed against seditious writers, and so thoroughly prejudiced the King's mind against Malesherbes that he brought about his banishment from Paris in 1771. Louis XVI. reinstated him in his office, appointing him Minister of the House, which was equivalent to being Secretary for the Home Department ; but when Turgot was dismissed from office Malesherbes resigned. 'I wish,' said Louis XVI. regretfully to him, ' that I too could resign my place.'

Malesherbes quietly passed the next sixteen years of his life in the country, but when Louis XVI. was brought to trial, he emerged from his retreat, and begged to be allowed to act as counsel for his former master and friend. It was not only a forlorn hope, but a dangerous request, as has been previously stated. When the King was sentenced to death Malesherbes' fortitude gave way, and he could only utter a few unintelligible words, broken with sobs. A year later he was arrested on the pretext of having conspired against the unity of the Republic, and as he declined to offer any defence, he was at once ordered to be executed. Not content with taking his life, the Tribunal sent with him to the guillotine his daughter,

Madame de Rosambo, and his daughter-in-law, Madame de Chateaubriand, the sister-in-law of the great writer. As Malesherbes was leaving his prison on the way to the scaffold his foot struck a stone. 'This is a bad omen,' he said with grim irony ; 'a Roman would have turned back.'

On 27th June 1794 the guillotine cut short the career of Henri Linguet, one of the most famous lawyers and writers of the eighteenth century. His sarcastic wit, his querulous temper, and paradoxical turn of mind constantly brought him into trouble. Among the great personages he offended was the Duc de Duras, who, though he had never commanded an army, had been made a Marshal, and though he had never written a book, was elected to the Academy. The Duke had been thus promoted to the highest military honours with six other officers at the coronation of Louis XVI., and the seven new Marshals were compared by Linguet to the seven deadly sins, explaining that they could not be compared to the seven planets, as Mars was not to be found among them. The Duke threatened to have Linguet thrashed with a truncheon. 'M. le Maréchal,' he replied, 'you are not in the habit of using it.' In 1779 Linguet's enemies succeeded in having him sent to the Bastille. On entering his cell he was alarmed at the sight of a tall gaunt man. 'Who are you?' he asked.

Henri Linguet, 1736-1794.

'I am the barber of the Bastille,' answered the man. 'Then you ought to have shaved it away,' rejoined Linguet, much relieved. Linguet was kept two years in confinement, and on his release wrote his 'Memoirs of the Bastille,' which made a deep impression on the public. An ingenious pamphlet on the Netherlands brought him to the notice of the Emperor Joseph II., who invited him to Vienna, and munificently rewarded and ennobled him. Linguet, however, unable to restrain the spirit of opposition that characterised all his actions and writings, took the part of the inhabitants of Brabant in their rebellion against the Emperor, which resulted in his expulsion from Austria. In his earlier years, to annoy his friends the Encyclopædists, he had written a vindication of Nero and a defence of despotism. This production was fated to cost him dear, and, true to his invariable disposition, when the Convention met he attacked its most influential members. He went into hiding during the Reign of Terror, but was discovered, brought before the Revolutionary Tribunal, and condemned to death for having 'offered up incense to despots,' and was executed the same day.

Many personal friends of Louis XVI. and members of the Court had sought safety in flight during the progress of the Revolution, but there were many who had remained in Paris or its neighbourhood, either from a contemptuous indifference to the danger that menaced them or in the belief that they would be left unmolested in their seclusion ; others again were too aged or infirm to travel. Sooner or later they were all undeceived in their illusions or hopes. The Duc de Mouchy had retired to his château near Paris after the imprisonment of the King, but having afforded a refuge to some recalcitrant priests, he was arrested by the emissaries of the Tribunal and taken to prison, whither he was at once followed by his wife—Marie Antoinette's ' Madame Etiquette.' On being told there was no warrant out against her, she replied, ' My husband's arrest implies mine.' She insisted on accompanying him when he was summoned before the Tribunal, and on being informed that she had not been ordered to come, she again said, ' The order for my husband's appearance also implies mine.' When she heard that her husband had been sentenced to death and that she was not implicated in the sentence, she said for the third time, ' My husband's condemnation also implies mine.' When she was arraigned the clerk informed the presiding judge that she could not hear what was said, being deaf, a difficulty which the latter functionary surmounted by ordering the jury to find that ' she had conspired deafly.' As he was leaving the prison one of his companions in affliction exhorted the veteran Marshal to be courageous, and he turned on his friend

Philippe de Noailles, Maréchal, Duc de Mouchy, 1715-1794.

and said, 'When I was seventeen years of age I mounted to the assault for my King ; now that I am nearly eighty I shall mount the scaffold for my God. I am not to be pitied.'   The same cart that conveyed the Duc and Duchesse de Mouchy to the guillotine contained their sister-in-law, the Duchesse de Noailles, their daughter-in-law, the Duchesse d'Ayen, and grand-daughter, the Vicomtesse de Noailles. The Tribunal was not addicted to half-measures.

Madame Lavergne, the wife of the Commander of Longwy, was no less heroic than the Duchesse de Mouchy. After the surrender of Longwy to the Duke of Brunswick in 1792 General Lavergne was sent to prison, though he was able to prove that he had been forced to capitulate by the Municipality. He was to be tried by court-martial, but the court never sat, and after having been kept fifteen months in confinement he was sent to the Revolutionary Tribunal, and condemned to death. When the verdict was given, a voice in the court cried out, 'Long live the King !' At once the order was given to seize the person who had dared to defy the Tribunal, and it proved to be Madame Lavergne. On being arrested, she declared that she only wished to share her husband's fate, and knew no other means of achieving her purpose. It is needless to say that the judge complied with her desire.

Robespierre.

About the same time there perished the Duchesse de Gramont, sister of the Duc de Choiseul, the Minister of Louis XV. She was taken before the Tribunal with her friend, the Duchesse du Châtelet, whom, at the peril of her own life, she had vainly tried to save. Asked whether it was true that she had sent money to assist the émigrés, she answered after a pause, ' I was tempted to deny it, but my life is not worth a lie.' While the Duchesse de Gramont was in prison some members of the Committee of Public Safety called on her more than once, and hinted that she would be pardoned if she consented to disclose the asylum of her friend's son, the Comte du Châtelet. ' To turn informer,' she disdainfully replied, ' is too new a civic virtue for me to be able to practise it.'

Beatrice de Choiseul, Duchesse de Gramont, 1730-1794.

Danton's death was the prelude to wholesale executions in Paris, which, however, soon disgusted the middle classes. The guillotine had to be removed to the distant Barrière du Trône, on the road to Vincennes, and was kept at work there, indiscriminately thinning the prisons of suspected aristocrats and the Convention of unsuspected patriots. The surviving deputies became alarmed, for the life of the most sincere Republican was no longer secure from the wild blood-craving of the Committee of Public Safety. Robespierre had ceased to be a member of it, but he had himself drawn up a law which was passed on the 10th of June, and which, under

Maximilien de Robespierre, 1759-1794.

the guise of improving the organisation of the Revolutionary Tribunal, invested it with the most terrible powers. The accused were no longer allowed to have counsel ; preliminary investigations, written depositions, and the hearing of witnesses were abolished. To 'speak ill' of a patriot, or to 'corrupt the morals' of one was to be 'an enemy of the people,' and what this meant was but too clear. Any member of the Convention might be arraigned before the bar of the Tribunal without a preliminary vote authorising his arrest. The Convention was seized with terror, and there were sixty of its members who no longer dared to spend the night in their homes, fearing that at any moment they might be arrested. But Robespierre had overshot the mark. On the eve of reaching the goal of his ambition he was consigned to the same fate as the countless victims he had allowed to be sacrificed.

The character of Robespierre has often been elaborately and conscientiously analysed, but his career was so strange and his nature so complex that the judgments which have been passed upon him are as opposed to each other as were his acts to his principles. Like most of the leaders of the Revolution, he was a lawyer. At the age of twenty-four he was appointed a judge in his native town of Arras, and was at that time particularly distinguished for clemency. Being obliged to sentence a man to death, he resigned, and thenceforward he devoted himself exclusively to practising at the Bar. His sister, with whom he lived, seeing that he was stung with remorse for having taken the life of a fellow-creature, tried in vain to console him, saying that he had only meted out justice to a base criminal. 'No doubt he was an infamous wretch,' replied Robespierre, 'still I have been the cause of the death of a man.' Being accomplished, cultured, and eloquent, Robespierre shone for some years in the society of Arras, discussing with his friends Rousseau's theories, by which he was captivated, and in which he believed to the end of his days. The summoning of the States-General deprived the Bar of Arras of its chief ornament, as Robespierre was elected deputy for the province of Artois. He now became absorbed in politics, and took a prominent part in the debates in the Assembly. 'That man will go far,' said Mirabeau of him; and in many ways Robespierre went farther than he could have ever expected. He who had wept over the death of a criminal voted for the death of his King, on which occasion he said to the Convention, 'You are not judges, but statesmen; you have not merely to pass sentence on a single man, but to take measures for the public safety. Louis must die so that the country may live.' In judging a public man allowance must be made for the conditions in which he is placed, and the national interests that are at stake, to which he may be forced to subordinate his personal inclinations. No doubt the life of Louis XVI. was a constant menace to the security of the country and to Republican institutions ; and Robespierre was a fanatical Republican. On these grounds the vote he gave for the King's death may be explained, but his acquiescence in the murder of the Girondists, and the slaughter of thousands of innocent persons at a time when the Republic had nothing to fear from them, cannot be explained or condoned on any ground. From the merciful man he once was, he was converted with singular rapidity into the most bloodthirsty ; and for one who laboured in the cause of 'Liberty, Equality, and Fraternity,' it was, to say the least, inconsistent to strive, as he so plainly did, for the attainment of power. He was not an atheist, yet he was at the head of the atheistical party ; to the last day of his life he was in every sense a fop, employed the most elaborate and studied language, wore knee-breeches and silk stockings, and had his hair powdered, yet he was the leader of the 'sans-culottes.' A deist and religious in feeling, he made a compromise with his conscience by substituting the worship of 'a Supreme Being,' with the dogma of the immortality of the soul, for the semi-pagan cult of the Goddess of Reason. But the ceremony with which the new worship was inaugurated was as idolatrous in its form as were the rites of the one that preceded it, being in fact a grotesque medley of theatrical and profane pomp. While walking with the official body at the inauguration of the new religious rites, Robespierre drew to the front and placed himself at the head of his colleagues, thereby asserting his superior position over them. The hint was not thrown away, and the most influential members of the Convention, led by Tallien, entered into a conspiracy against the man whom they believed was aiming at a dictatorship. Robespierre now gave them the opportunity they desired to bring their plot to a head. On 26th July he read to the Convention a long and carefully prepared speech, in which, on the one hand, he proposed that the Reign of Terror should be ended, and on the other, declared that many of the deputies deserved punishment. But who was to be punished? Whose head was to fall next? The whole Assembly trembled at the threats which Robespierre uttered in clear, angry tones. On the following day, the 9th Thermidor according to the Republican calendar, Billaud opened the debate and impeached Robespierre in violent language, winding up with the words, 'The Assembly stands between two alternative butcheries, and it will perish if it shows any weakness.' Then Tallien drew forth a dagger, and making a theatrical oration, swore that he would stab himself if the new Cromwell were allowed to triumph. Robespierre rushed to the tribune, but was assailed from all sides with the cry, 'Down with the tyrant!' Livid with rage, he turned to the side of the Chamber where the Moderate party sate. 'It is you,' he shouted, 'you, the pure men, I address, not these brigands.' Not being able to continue owing to the uproar, he cried out at the President—'President of assassins, for the last time I ask leave to speak!' The confusion had now reached its height, and one voice was heard to exclaim, 'The blood of Danton chokes you!' 'Down with the tyrant!' cried the whole Assembly, and Robespierre and his associates were impeached, seized, and sent to the prison of the Luxembourg. Meanwhile the Commune had risen, and Paris was in a state of insurrection. Robespierre was released from arrest, and fled to the Hotel de Ville, which was attacked during the night. In the fray he was shot at by a constable named Merda,[1] and fell on a table, his jaw broken by the bullet. He was taken to the Conciergerie, where he asked for a pen.—'Is it to write to your Supreme Being?' mockingly inquired the jailer; 'it is not worth while, for you will soon go to see him.' On the following day, with his face bandaged and disfigured, and suffering excruciating pain, he was conveyed with twenty-one of his friends to the Place de la Révolution, where the guillotine had been re-erected for the special purpose

[1] Or, as some say, shot himself.

of his execution. He died without attempting to speak, though he roared like a tiger when the executioner seized him and tore off the bandage from his head. His sister Charlotte, whom he had generously supported while he resided at Arras, afterwards lived with him for a short time in Paris. She vainly tried to see her brother while he was in the Conciergerie, and after his execution was herself thrown into prison, but was soon liberated. Napoleon allowed her a pension of three thousand five hundred francs, which both Louis XVIII. and Charles X. continued to give her. She died in 1834.

It is fruitless to attempt to draw a line between the cant and hypocrisy of which Robespierre may be accused and the purity or sincerity of his motives. A man's motives may be perfectly honest, but however much he parades them they are of no account in the evolution of history, in which his actions only tell. Some of Robespierre's motives were worthy of respect, as they sprang from a genuine interest and trust in the people, and in his desire to found a constitution on the broadest popular basis. But while wishing to give effect to Rousseau's ideal theories of socialism and equal division of property, he failed to perceive that justice, security, and confidence are the essentials of good government and stability. He may be pardoned by some for the means he employed in the pursuit of his objects, but it would be idle to ignore that while labouring on behalf of the people he was aiming at supremacy for himself, to gain which end he transgressed every law of humanity. What form his supremacy might have eventually taken he probably knew himself as little as it is possible for us to surmise. Fate forced him to become a man of action, when by nature he was only a doctrinaire. Here, in part, lies the clue to his failure. He was fearless of death, but lacked the intrepid initiative which defies peril and commands success. His humanity has often been commended, and it has been alleged, not without some plausibility, that he had no direct hand in many of the excesses of the Terror, whose atrocities he unquestionably desired to terminate. However, whether he inspired them or not, as a rule he expressed approval of the shedding of blood after it had been shed,—as in the case of the September massacres—and was, therefore, if not an instigator, an accomplice after the fact. That he could be also an instigator of crime on a colossal scale was proved by his signing, on the 20th of June, a list of 138 persons whom the Committee of Public Safety sent to the Revolutionary Tribunal. It has been contended, too, that he had not the power to stay the revolutionary fury, and was obliged to submit to the force of circumstances. But that he had the power, when he chose to exercise it, was exemplified by the two episodes of Catherine Théot and Cécile Rénault.

Catherine Théot was an old woman, whose reason had almost been unhinged by the excitement of the times, and who, with a band of equally hysterical followers, proclaimed that she herself was the Virgin Mary and that Robespierre was the Messiah. The Convention ordered her to be prosecuted, but, in spite of its orders, she was released by the Public Accuser through the influence of Robespierre. Cécile Rénault was an ignorant, uneducated, vain girl, whose wits were as much obscured by political excitement as were those of Catherine Théot. Her father, a poor stationer, forbade her to go out alone, but one day she slipped away unnoticed, and called to see Robespierre, who chanced to be out. Two of Robespierre's friends were passing by at the time, and observing the young girl's annoyance at not finding him at home, questioned her, and being struck by the strangeness of her replies, took her off to the Committee of Public Safety. She calmly answered the interrogatories there addressed to her, and said she wanted to see Robespierre, ' to know what a tyrant looked like.' She had a package in her hand which contained some clothing. ' I brought these things with me so that I might have a change,' she explained. ' Why ? ' they asked ; ' where did you think you would be taken ? ' ' To prison, and then

to the guillotine,' was her answer. On being
searched, two small penknives were found in her
pocket—presents from her relations. She was
sent at once to the Conciergerie.

On the same day that Cécile Rénault made
her unfortunate call at Robespierre's house, a
man named Admiral had attempted the life of
Collot d'Herbois, and was caught in the act.
Robespierre saw at once the opportunity that
the coincidence of these two occurrences gave
him, and he took advantage of it with consummate cunning and cruelty for the furtherance of
his personal aims. For some time the Committee
of Public Safety had been aware that the Baron
de Batz, formerly a Royalist Deputy to the
National Assembly, was engaged in some vague
conspiracy against the Republic. De Batz
was a man of mysterious and shady character,
of whom but little is known even now. He
had previously signalised himself by planning
the rescue of Louis XVI. on his way to execution, and by plotting to deliver Marie Antoinette
from prison. He was possessed of ample means
—though it is not clear how he obtained them—
which he employed to set his conspiracy against
the Republic on foot, and he bribed a couple of
Deputies to assist in executing the plot. One
of these, an unfrocked monk named Chabot,
who led a disreputable life, was arrested and
guillotined, but de Batz successfully eluded the
search of Robespierre's spies. It is possible that

*Baron de
Batz,
1760-1822.*

Admiral may have been hired by one of de
Batz's accomplices, though he was ignorant of
any general conspiracy, and there was no doubt
whatever of Cécile Rénault's entire innocence
of the crime laid at her door. Robespierre,
however, was not the man to be daunted by a
trifle of that kind, so he caused the report to be
circulated that Admiral and Cécile Rénault were
concerned in a vast conspiracy whose object was
the overthrow of the Republic. To impress
the minds of the people with the enormity of
the alleged crime in being directed against the
State as personified by himself, he arranged that
a considerable number of persons should be
selected from the prisons in which they were
confined, and that they should be arraigned with
Cécile Rénault and Admiral before the Revolutionary Tribunal, as being incriminated in the
conspiracy.

At ten o'clock on a hot morning early in
June 1794, fifty-four persons of all ranks and
ages were brought before the Tribunal—ladies,
workgirls, dukes, princes, artisans, gendarmes,
and domestics—a motley crowd, including Cécile
Rénault's brother, father, and aunt. Some few
of them had been slightly acquainted with
de Batz, but, with the exception of Admiral,
there was not a tittle of evidence against any
of them of any knowledge of or participation
in the alleged conspiracy. But Robespierre
knew well enough that the Tribunal cared

very little whether the prisoners it pretended to try were guilty or not. 'Have you attempted the life of the representative of the people?' was the only question put by Dumas,[1] the President, in turn to each of the accused. 'I have but one regret,' replied Admiral, 'that I missed that scoundrel Collot!' 'I never had any intention of killing Robespierre,' said Cécile Rénault, 'I merely considered him one of my country's greatest tyrants.' The others simply answered 'No' to the question. Fouquier-Tinville and Dumas then briefly addressed the jury, who, having deliberated for half-an-hour, returned a verdict of guilty. It took four hours to 'make the toilette' of the condemned; the doors of the Conciergerie were then thrown open, and the mob yelled at the prisoners, who were just sallying forth when the order was given to wait. Fouquier-Tinville had but now remembered that each of them was to be clothed in the red shirt of the parricide, and the unhappy men and women were kept in mortal suspense for another long hour, while the scarlet robes were being made in which they were sent to execution. They arrived at last at the foot of the guillotine at seven o'clock in the evening. Michelet relates that a man known for his colossal strength and iron nerve betted

---

[1] President Dumas, who was no relative of General Dumas, the father of the famous novelist, was guillotined after Thermidor.

that he would stand by and see the executions from first to last without faltering. For some time he unflinchingly bore the sight, but when a young girl named Nichole, a mere child, stepped forward, lay down on the plank, and gently asked the executioner, 'Am I right this way?' his brain reeled and he dropped in a dead faint.

It is clear that in snatching Catherine Théot from the clutches of the Convention, Robespierre's guiding motive was to save the woman whose crazy adulation flattered his vanity; while in destroying Cécile Rénault, and in investing her death with such gruesome accompaniments, he emphasised his pretensions to be considered the head of the State, and as such the special object of attack by its enemies. Robespierre was successful so long as he played the game of the revolutionary leaders with whom he was associated. He dominated the all-powerful Jacobin Club by his violent but carefully studied rhetoric and his able advocacy of its subversive views, while, by assenting to the sacrifice of unoffending young girls and old men, he gratified the taste of the mob. But there were men whom he had spared, or whose doom he had deferred—men who were far stronger and cleverer than he was, and they, after his murder of Danton, as soon as he threatened the Convention itself and tried to strike out a line of his own, turned upon him and put an end to his monstrous career. Robespierre proved by his acts that he was domestic, virtuous, and incorruptible, but he proved by them also that he was narrow-minded, incompetent, and weak. He could only destroy, he could not construct, was carried away by the popular storm he had assisted in raising, and fell the very day he attempted to control it.

The Revolution of Thermidor burst so unexpectedly on Robespierre and his friends that they had not time to guard themselves from the attack. Its sudden explosion was mainly due to the action of Tallien. At first Tallien may have been impelled to join the conspirators by personal considerations, but he was afterwards urged on by worthier motives. His reputed father was the steward of the Marquis de Bercy. The Marquis took an interest in the quick-witted lad, who was supposed in reality to be his own son, procuring him a clerkship in a notary's office. But when the Revolution broke out Tallien left his desk, took to journalism, and, having become a member of the Jacobin Club, entered the Convention. He was one of those on whose advice, or by whose command, the attack on the Tuileries on 10th August was made, and at whose instigation the September massacres took place. At Bordeaux, where he was sent to organise the Reign of Terror, he displayed a homicidal mania equal

Jean Lambert Tallien, 1769-1820.

to that shown by Lebon at Arras and Carrier
at Nantes. But on an auspicious day for
himself and his prisoners, he met the Marquise
de Fontenay, who had been proscribed by the
Committee of Public Safety, and was flying
to Madrid. Madame de Fontenay was beautiful, and Tallien was young and ardent. He
fell passionately in love with her, and to
gain her affections he became merciful, while
to save her own life Madame de Fontenay
yielded to him. She soon secured the release of
many prisoners, and the guillotine at Bordeaux
slackened in its work. But Commissioners were
not sent out by the Convention to exercise
clemency. Tallien was recalled to Paris. His
life was spared. Great as was the popularity
of Robespierre he dared not attack the man
who had been elected President of the Convention, and who presided over it at the most
critical period of its existence—during the trial
of Danton. But to punish the soft-hearted
proconsul in the way calculated to hurt him
most, Robespierre ordered Madame de Fontenay to be sent to prison. Her liberty was
then offered to her, provided she would declare
that Tallien had betrayed the Republic at
Bordeaux. ‘I am only twenty,’ she replied
to Robespierre’s emissary, ‘but I should prefer
to die twenty times over!’ In consequence
of her refusal she was thrown into a foul
dungeon with damp straw for a bed, and was

Thérèse Cabarrus, Marquise de Fontenay, 1775-1836.

transferred three times from prison to prison, until at last Robespierre ordered her to be guillotined, little imagining that the weapon with which he proposed to strike her down would be turned upon himself.

On the 4th of Thermidor Tallien found a dagger on his table. How had it come there? Who had brought it? No one had been seen coming into the room, which he had only left for half-an-hour. He recognised the dagger as being Madame de Fontenay's. It was a mute but eloquent appeal. On the 7th Thermidor a letter reached him from Madame de Fontenay in prison, in which she wrote: 'I have just been informed that to-morrow I appear before the Revolutionary Tribunal, which means the scaffold. This does not correspond with a dream I had last night, in which I fancied that Robespierre had ceased to exist, and my prison doors were unlocked. Thanks to your cowardice, soon there will be no one left in France to fulfil my dream.' Maddened with passion, Tallien hastened the execution of the plot, and Madame de Fontenay's dream came true to the letter. To reward her saviour she became his wife. For her good work at Bordeaux, Madame de Fontenay was called Our Lady of Mercy; in history Madame Tallien lives as Our Lady of Thermidor. Tallien took an active part in the events of next year, and during the Directory he was a member of the Council of the Five Hundred. Nevertheless he was shunned by the Royalists for the part he had played in the Revolution, and by the Republicans because they considered him a renegade. He was even forsaken by his wife, who had never been sincerely devoted to him, and who obtained a divorce to marry the Prince de Chimay. Napoleon, who was under some obligation to Tallien, took him to Egypt; on his return he fell into the hands of the English, and was brought to London, where society, remembering his action on the 9th Thermidor, welcomed him with open arms. On leaving England the Duchess of Devonshire sent him her portrait set in diamonds. Tallien, who was so poor that he could not pay for his lodgings, kept the portrait, but returned the gems with a note of thanks, in which he said, 'Le cadre c'est votre esprit!' Later on he was appointed Consul at Alicante, where he lost an eye as the result of an attack of yellow fever, and in 1820 he died in Paris in complete obscurity and dire distress. It is said that shortly before his death he was visited in his humble dwelling by M. Decaze, one of his Ministers, by order of Louis XVIII. 'M. Tallien,' said the Minister, 'you know that his Majesty has forgotten everything.' 'I have forgotten nothing,' haughtily replied Tallien. 'I am certain that his Majesty would be glad to offer you a better house.' 'It is my own,' was

the answer ; ' were Louis XVIII. to offer me
the Tuileries and his civil list, I should refuse
them.   I am weaned from the splendours of this
world, and am happy to die forgotten.   The
idols I once worshipped are broken, but they
are still my creed.   My place now is in the
grave—and in history.'   It is impossible not to
feel some sympathy with Tallien, for the part
he filled in the dramatic episode of the climax
of the Revolution, for the glamour shed on his
earlier years by the beauty of a celebrated woman,
his lamentable downfall from a high position,
and his republican stoicism—all of which invest
his career with the glow of romance.

In accordance with Madame de Fontenay's
dream, the day after the fall of Robespierre the
prison doors were opened and the proceedings
of the Revolutionary Tribunal were suspended.
The Terrorists were overwhelmed by the sudden
turn of the tide.   Yet, while eighty-two sup-
porters of Robespierre—chiefly members of the
Commune—were guillotined at once, and shortly
afterwards Carrier and Lebon, and subsequently
many others of their kind suffered the same fate,
Collot, Billaud, and Barère, the three most bloodthirsty members of the Committee of Public
Safety, were only sentenced to transportation ;
and of these, Barère was liberated after a short
term of imprisonment in a fortress.

Jean Collot   Collot had been despatched by the Revolution
d'Herbois,
1751-1796. to quell the insurrection at Lyons.   ' The justice

of the Republic,' he said, 'should strike like
lightning. Our sensitiveness is all on behalf of
the country ; those who know us will appreciate
our devotion. In smiting miscreants to death
we ensure the lives of generations of freemen.'
To make good his words, and the guillotine not
being expeditious enough to 'strike like lightning,' he poured volleys of musketry on the
prisoners, shooting them down in hundreds, and
then razing their homes to the ground.

Billaud during the September massacres egged
on the assassins in their work. Some apologists
of the Revolution have asserted that these
massacres were the outcome of a sudden frenzy
of a small portion of the mob, and that they
were neither instigated nor approved by the
leaders of the democracy. Documents in the
National Library, which have recently come to
light, show, however, that the responsibility for
them rests, indirectly if not directly, on some of
the most influential members of the National
Assembly and the Commune. The massacres ex-
tended over six days, and had they not been coun-
tenanced by the governing authorities, and wilfully ignored by the National Assembly which was
sitting at the time, they could have been stopped
at once. That they were premeditated was evi-
dent from the fact that they were carried out on
a systematic plan organised by the Commune,
who hired and paid the assassins for their work.
'You need not rob these scoundrels,' said Billaud

J. Nicholas Billaud-Varennes, 1762-1819.

R

to the butchers as they rifled the bodies of the aristocrats, ' you will be paid as has been agreed.'

Bertrand Barère, ✝ *1755-1841.* Barère advocated or connived at every infamous act that was sanctioned by the Convention and the Committee of Public Safety. ' The chameleon of the Revolution,' as he has been called, he belonged to every party and denounced every party in turn, always calling for the extreme penalty of the law to be applied to his colleagues or associates when their star was on the wane. This excessive zeal on behalf of the ' Republic' was censured even by Robespierre, who reproved him for the gratuitous murder of Marie Antoinette, as had Barère not sent her to the Revolutionary Tribunal the Queen's life might have been spared.

Antoine Fouquier-Tinville, 1747-1795. Yet ferocious as was Collot, savage as was Billaud, and infamous as was Barère, Fouquier-Tinville, the Public Accuser, was more ferocious, more savage, and more infamous still. He first brought himself into notice by a poem which he dedicated to Louis XVI. But as his lyrics met with scant appreciation from the public, he found a more congenial and profitable occupation for his genius as a police spy. The outbreak of the Revolution afforded him a yet wider scope for the exercise of his talents. He joined the Commune, and distinguished himself in the ' insurrection of the sections.' So active and useful a member of society could not escape the notice of Danton and Robespierre, and shortly after the

10th of August they appointed him Public Accuser. He had the power to arrest and accuse before the Revolutionary Tribunal whomsoever he chose to lay hands upon ; he not only drew up the indictment and conducted the prosecution, but ordered the executioner to carry out the sentence of death. His opportunity had now come. He was the right man in the right place. He threw himself into his work with unparalleled ardour and zest, making arrests indiscriminately day and night, so that the Revolutionary Tribunal should not flag in its labours, lying so that his victims should not escape. During the seventeen months he was in office over 2000 persons appeared before the Tribunal, and not once did he speak in favour of an accused person. He was so sure of the verdicts, that the carts in which the prisoners were to be conveyed to execution were brought to the door before the death sentence had been delivered. One day he erected the guillotine in the very hall of the Tribunal, but he was induced to remove it when Collot represented to him that ' it would demoralise the executions.' In order to expedite the proceedings further, he induced the judges to condemn the accused in batches, and in one instance he brought as many as 160 prisoners before the judges together. But in this proceeding he went too far, as a rule was laid down providing that not more than 60 were to be arraigned at one time.

Fouquier-Tinville's agents seem to have been imbued with all their master's reckless disregard for the value of human life. One of them went to the prison of the Luxembourg one morning with a list of eighteen prisoners who were to be brought before the Tribunal, but only seventeen could be found at hand. 'What shall I do?' he anxiously inquired of the jailer. 'Fouquier-Tinville told me to bring him eighteen anti-Revolutionists—I need one more to make up the number.' At that moment an ill-fated suspect happened to appear in sight. The agent asked his name, and though it was not that of the man who was wanted, he said, 'All right, you will do,' had him removed by the gendarmes with the others and guillotined at noon the same day. On another occasion an agent of the Public Accuser went to the prison for a man of fifty years of age. The intended victim, however, was in no hurry to answer, but a lad of seventeen, who was playing ball in the gallery, hearing the name called, and it being something like his own, asked whether he was wanted. The warder inquired his name, and on hearing it, said, 'Yes, you just come with me.' The youth was handed over to the agent, was taken to the Conciergerie, and was guillotined that afternoon in place of the man of fifty.

Of all the cases that came before the Tribunal none was more iniquitously dealt with than that which is now famous as that of the 'Virgins of

Verdun.' Verdun had surrendered to the Prussians on 2nd September 1792, but was re-taken by the French in the following month. A commission was then formed in the town by the so-called representatives of the people ' to search for the enemies of the Revolution and the Republic.' This Commission at once sent a large number of Royalists to prison, and called upon all good citizens ' to denounce the authors, abettors, and accomplices of the crimes which had been committed against the State.' Thirty-five persons who were accused of these crimes were kept eighteen months in prison at Verdun, and were then forwarded to the Conciergerie in Paris. These prisoners included seven young girls, the eldest of whom at the time of their alleged offence was twenty-four and the youngest fifteen years old, the remainder being men and women of all ages, ranging from forty to seventy-five. They had been accused by the Commissioners of having (1) congratulated the King of Prussia on his entry into Verdun ; (2) of having given a ball to the officers of the invading army ; (3) of having sent a deputation of seven young girls to the camp of the King to express their joy at his success. All that was proved by the inquiry was that though a few persons had gone to the Prussian camp, the King had received one middle-aged lady only, and merely asked her whether there was a theatre at Verdun ; that another lady had purchased a box of sweetmeats for the King, but had never delivered it, and, finally, that two of the youngest of the accused girls had handed over a sum of 2000 francs to a returned and impecunious émigré. Nevertheless, the thirty-five prisoners, after a preliminary investigation by one of the judges of the Tribunal,—who, in order not to waste his precious time, contented himself with an interview with them of five minutes' duration,—were brought before the Revolutionary Tribunal on 17th March 1794. On explaining to Fouquier-Tinville that the triumphal car which it was said had been sent to the Prussian camp was an old farm cart used for the conveyance of hay or manure, and contained only two young girls and an old man, the Public Accuser called out, 'Well, now I am able to appreciate the true worth of those fawning women, for that cart never carried more manure than it did when it took them to visit the tyrant.' There was not an atom of proof against any of the accused on any other point. Nothing could incriminate them but their own confession, but each, in order to screen the others, assumed the sole responsibility for what had been done. The audience was deeply touched by this spectacle of unselfish heroism, but nothing could move Fouquier-Tinville. At the end of his examination, the judge, a worthy compeer of the Public Accuser, put only one question to the jury. He asked them whether each of the accused was guilty of high treason. On receiving an answer in the affirmative, he condemned them all to death, with the exception of the two youngest girls, who were ordered first to be put in the pillory for six hours, bearing an inscription to the effect that they had handed over Verdun to the enemy, and to be afterwards sent to imprisonment for twenty years.

On the 14th Thermidor, five days after the execution of Robespierre, Fréron rose in the Convention and demanded the arrest of Fouquier-Tinville. He ended a long speech with the words, 'I ask that Fouquier should be sent to hell to sleep off the blood he has shed.' Fouquier was arrested and kept in prison for some months, when he was subjected to a lengthy trial. He pleaded his case with much skill and ingenuity, taking the stand that he had merely carried out the instructions he had received, and had incurred no personal responsibility. 'I have only been the hatchet of the Revolution,' he contended; 'how can you punish a hatchet?' The trial lasted forty-one days, and Fouquier must have wondered at the dilatoriness of the court. Finally, on 7th May 1794, he was sentenced to death, and was executed on the following morning in company with twelve other Terrorists. He met death bravely, with a 'marble brow,' according to the expression of a contemporary.[1] The mob hooted and jeered

[1] Mercier.

him—the same ungrateful mob that had hooted and jeered at the many hundreds of his victims whose execution they owed to his good offices.

France, after the 9th Thermidor, breathed freely again, and throughout the country there arose a cry of joy. Among the many persons whose lives were then spared were Madame de Beauharnais, the future Empress Josephine, and *Duchesse de* the Duchesse de Fleury, in whose honour her *Fleury,* fellow-prisoner, the poet André Chenier, had *1769-1820.* written his beautiful elegy, ' La Jeune Captive,' but who, less fortunate than the companion of his captivity, was executed on the 8th Thermidor. Soon after her release, the Duchesse de Fleury was divorced and married again. Napoleon in later years at an interview curtly asked her, ' Are you still as fond of men as you were ?' ' Yes, sire,' she replied, ' when they are civil.' Most of the leading men of the Revolution had either perished or had been sent to brood over the new turn of events in the marshes of Cayenne. Amongst those who survived was *Lazare* Carnot, a member of the Committee of Public *Nicholas* *Marguerite* Safety and War Minister — perhaps the most *Carnot,* energetic and capable War Minister France has *1753-1823.* ever had. He was attacked in the Convention for having spoken on behalf of his former colleagues, and would have been arrested but for the impression made on that assembly by the exclamation of a member : ' Would you dare lay hands on the

man who organised victory for the armies of
the Republic?' Carnot, after having been a
member of the Directory, continued as Minister
of War under the Consulate, but had to resign
for having voted against the proposal to elect
Napoleon Consul for life. He voted also against
the bestowal of the Imperial dignity on the First
Consul, and then retired from the public stage.
In 1814 Louis XVIII. made him Minister of
the Interior, but on the return of the Bourbons
after the Hundred Days, Carnot was banished
from France. He died at Magdeburg in 1823.

Fouché was one of the few Terrorists who
lived to attain high honours and great wealth.
That he passed safely through the many crises
of the Revolution, though he rode perilously
high on the crest of the wave, was due to
his sagacity in keeping on good terms with
the rulers of the day, and his semi-prophetic
intuition in discovering the men of the future
and of ingratiating himself with them at the
right moment. If the opportunity demanded,
he turned upon them with cold-blooded
cynicism, sacrificing them with the most
profound indifference, and he committed the
most heinous crimes against humanity under
the pretext of serving the public interest.
Being gifted with an unequalled genius for
tortuous intrigue, he made himself indispensable
to every party as it rose, only to betray it again
when it was to his advantage to do so.

Joseph Fouché, 1754-1820.

His father, a sea captain at Nantes, sent him to study at the Oratories of his native place and of Paris. He afterwards earned his livelihood by teaching mathematics and philosophy in various provincial towns, amongst others at Arras, where he made the acquaintance of Robespierre. In 1789 he abandoned his clerical pursuits, married, became an advocate, and blossomed out into an enthusiastic democrat. He made little impression on the Convention, for he was not an eloquent speaker, but the words he used when called upon to give his vote during the trial of Louis XVI. made a stir. 'I did not expect,' he said, 'that I should have to pronounce any other judgment on the tyrant but that of death. It seems as if we were afraid of the courage we showed in abolishing the monarchy; we falter before the shadow of a king.' The Girondists were his personal friends, and he never liked Robespierre; but he foresaw the triumph of The Mountain, and with the stoicism of a Spartan he voted for the arrest of the Girondist party. When the Reign of Terror was decreed, he fulfilled with complete unconcern and implacable thoroughness the missions on which he was sent. In the Niévre he carried out the law against the Royalist 'suspects' with so much vigour that he soon crushed the insurrection. The former oratorian and half-priest was now the chief promoter of the anti-religious movement, proscribing religious emblems, sending the Church plate to the Convention to be melted down, and inscribing on the gates of the cemeteries, ' Death is eternal sleep.' From the Niévre he was sent with Collot to establish the authority of the Convention at Lyons. It has already been shown how Collot discharged his duties. Fouché was not second to him in proving his devotion to the Republic, and the joint efforts of the two Commissioners were so thoroughly successful that a deputy could truly exclaim in the Convention, ' Lyons no longer exists ! ' On his return to Paris Fouché passed through many crises, and it took all the suppleness of his nature to enable him to save his neck from the guillotine. He belonged to Danton's party, but by supporting Danton he provoked the animosity of Robespierre. To propitiate Robespierre he spoke in favour of Danton's arrest ; but Robespierre's suspicions were not easily allayed, and they continued to rankle in his mind though he promoted Fouché to the presidency of the Jacobin Club. Once, and once only, Fouché was imprudent. On 8th June 1794, on the occasion of the festivities in honour of the new worship of the ' Supreme Being,' he publicly remarked sarcastically on the prominent attitude Robespierre then assumed. Yet it may be surmised either that he already saw the signs of the approaching storm which some few weeks later destroyed Robespierre and his party, or that he was desirous of raising that storm so that he should not be one of the next victims of the Terror. But, for the time, he played a dangerous game, as Robespierre, on being told of Fouché's remarks, at once asked the Committee of Public Safety for his head. Fouché, however, was ready for the emergency. He won the confidence of every surviving member of the parties which Robespierre had decimated, and wormed himself into their favour. He pointed out to them the dangers of their position, and greatly assisted in forming the conspiracy of Thermidor with Collot, Billaud, Tallien, and the others, whom he deserted in due course, as soon as he no longer needed their support.

The subsequent career of Fouché belongs to a period of history with which it is not intended to deal here. It will be sufficient to say that he served under the Directory, the Consulate, the Empire, and the Restoration with the same adroitness as he had served during the Terror. He was faithful to each Government as long as it seemed likely to last, while carrying on intrigues with the one he foresaw would rise in its place. As Police Minister, a capacity in which he was employed many years, he has had no equal ; he has had few equals either, in his skill in fishing in dirty and troubled waters. Of his early associates it is but fair to say that they were conscientious at heart, and the excesses they committed were the result of blind fanaticism or mistaken patriotism. But not one of them can be charged with soiling his hands by taking a bribe, not one was open to corrupting influences, not one who did not risk, and, if necessary, forfeit his life for the principles he professed. Fouché from first to last thought solely of his own advancement and the gratification of his avarice. He had no conscience, no moral principle, no sense of honour or of patriotism; he renounced and persecuted the Church when atheism was the fashion; he became a Terrorist not through conviction, but to stand well with the Convention; he supported the Directory to be appointed a Minister; he counselled the *coup d'état* of Brumaire when he saw that the Directory was about to expire; and to earn the Emperor's gratitude he urged Napoleon to take the Crown. The Jacobin now became Duke of Otranto; but on the first symptom of the Emperor's downfall, he who had voted for the death of Louis XVI. betrayed Napoleon to the Bourbons. Louis XVIII. reinstated Fouché for a short time in his former office of Police Minister, and then, to remove the arch-conspirator out of his way, sent him as ambassador to Dresden. But Fouché soon had to resign, and he died at Trieste in 1820.

General Thiébault, a contemporary of Fouché, says that Napoleon distrusted and disliked the latter, and wishing to humble his Minister, walked up to him one day at Court and

said : 'You were an abbé once?' 'Yes, sire.'
'You voted for the death of Louis XVI.?'
added Napoleon. 'Yes, sire; it was the first
good office I rendered your Majesty,' was the
retort. Napoleon, adds Thiébault, never forgot
the reply, and Fouché never forgave the Emperor
the question which provoked it. Fouché, however, had never entered the Church, and was
never an abbé, so that only the second part
of this conversation, which has been corro-
borated by many writers, can be accepted as
authentic.

In all countries the Church has afforded to
men of great capacity, though of humble birth,
the means of rising to eminence. Cardinal
Maury would have been a great prelate at any
time, but were it not for the Revolution he might
not have become a historical character. He was
the son of a cobbler, and was born at Valreas in
the Comtat Venaissin. He was sent to a good
school, where he soon mastered the humanities ;
he then entered the seminary at Avignon, where
he gave proof of the possession of that extraordinary memory which in later years availed
him so well. On being reproved one day by
the superior of the institution for not having
attended at church, he replied that he had been
there. 'You were not,' replied his master, 'and
you would be sorely embarrassed if I were to ask
you the text on which the sermon was preached.'
'Well,' replied Maury, 'your question comes at

*Jean
Siffrein
Maury*,
1746-1817.

Cardinal Maury.

the right time. I had written the first half of
the sermon from memory, and had begun the
other when you called me '—an assertion he
was able to substantiate. When barely twenty
Maury left for Paris, with only a few francs
in his pocket, and without any letters of introduction. It is said that while travelling
on the coach he engaged in conversation
with two young adventurers like himself,
one of whom was going to be a medical
student, the other a lawyer. The first vaunt-
ingly said, 'I shall become a member of the
Academy of Science and Physician to the King.'
' And I Advocate-General,' continued the other
with equal confidence. ' As for me,' said Maury,
' I shall become Preacher to the King, and an
Academician.' The medical student was Portal,
who was eventually elected a member of the
Academy of Science, and became Physician to
Louis XVIII. ; the law student, Treilhard, was
subsequently a member of the Committee of
Public Safety, of the Directory, an Imperial
Senator, and in the end was created a Count.

Maury maintained himself in Paris by giving lessons to young pupils, and he also wrote
some books which procured him an eulogium
from the Academy. When he was ordained his
eloquence as a preacher drew such crowds to hear
him that the Academy invited him to preach in
their chapel ; and as his fame reached the ears
of Louis XVI., he was commanded to deliver a

sermon at Versailles. His ambition was now gratified, yet but for that presence of mind which never failed him, he might have made a fatal step.   In the course of his sermon he ventured to tell some home truths which offended the Court ; but on perceiving the impression they made, he added adroitly, ' And so spoke St. Jean Chrysostome.'   In 1785 he became a member of the Academy, and in 1789 a representative of the clergy in the States-General.   In the Assembly, where he was welcomed for his eloquence, he determined to shine as a political orator, and decided at once to take up the foremost position as the defender of the privileges of the clergy and the nobility. ' I have been watching the struggle between the parties,' he said, ' and I am resolved to die in the breach, though, alas! I feel sure the place will be taken by storm and sacked.'   Maury's prophecy proved in part true.   The old *régime* was taken and sacked; but he did not die in the breach. After the fall of the Bastille, hearing that his life was threatened, he attempted to escape from the country.   But he was foiled, and was obliged to return to his place in the Assembly, where he engaged in a long and brilliant encounter with Mirabeau.   Thus the singular spectacle was presented of the son of a cobbler defending the privileged orders, while the son of a noble was championing the cause of the people.   Maury's magnificent presence, his graceful gestures, his

splendid voice, and his thrilling eloquence made
him a fitting match for his formidable opponent,
who one day, as he was about to reply to one of
Maury's happiest efforts, excitedly told him, ' I
shall now drive you into a vicious circle.' ' Is
it because you wish us to meet?' quietly replied
the Abbé. His speeches often provoked an
uproar, but that never disturbed him. During
a debate on the civil constitution of the clergy,
in which he had taken a leading part, he said,
' The tumult of this Assembly may smother my
voice, but it will not smother the truth.' On
another occasion, as his voice was lost in the
hubbub some ladies were making in the gallery,
he turned to the President and sarcastically said,
' Sir, please silence these *sans-culottes*,' thus coin-
ing a famous word, which the Revolution, however, applied in a different sense from the one he
intended. Owing to the opinions which he
fearlessly expressed, Maury was very unpopular,
and but for the readiness of his wit he would
have paid dearly for his temerity. On leaving
the Assembly on one occasion he was surrounded
by an angry mob, who shouted out at him, ' To
the lantern! to the lantern!' ' Do you think
if you hang me there that it will give any better
light?' he banteringly answered, and the mob
dispersed laughing. On another occasion a wild
ruffian brandished a cutlass at him, and threatened
to 'send him to say mass to the devil.' ' All
right,' rejoined the Abbé, ' you shall be my

assistant ; here are my cruets,' and he pointed a pair of pistols at the man. Again the mob laughed and cheered. One day, meeting a pedlar who, to advertise his wares by attracting attention to himself, was crying out, 'The death of the Abbé Maury,' the Abbé gave him a sound box on the ear and said, 'If I am dead you should at least believe in ghosts.' At the end of 1791 Maury, finding that all efforts to defend or save the old order were fruitless, emigrated to Rome, where the Pope gave him a bishopric, and then raised him to the Cardinalate. The exiled Louis XVIII. appointed him Ambassador to the Holy See, but shortly after the proclamation of the Empire, Maury rallied to the side of Napoleon, returned to France, and was made Archbishop of Paris. By accepting this dignity he estranged the Pope, who was then the Emperor's prisoner at Savona, and also Louis XVIII., who at the Restoration had him expelled from the Academy. In 1814 he returned to Rome, but was imprisoned by the Pope in the castle of St. Angelo, an imprisonment which cost him his life, as he died in 1817, a broken-hearted man, from a disease he had contracted there. To the last he retained the coolness with which he had attacked Mirabeau, and the ready wit which had saved him from being torn to pieces by the Paris mob. 'You value yourself very highly,' said M. Regnaud de St. Jean d'Angely, the Imperial Secretary of

State, to him, when Maury was defending himself
haughtily from an attack on his political conduct.
—'Not in my own estimation, but I do when I
compare myself to others,' he replied scornfully.

From the very outset to the close of the
Revolution, one man persistently endeavoured *Abbé Siéyes,* 1748-1836.
to establish the Republic on a permanent basis
by devoting his great capacity to drawing up
schemes for a constitution. Siéyes was born at
Frèjus, and though he wished to become a soldier,
was forced to enter the Church. He was rapidly
promoted to high ecclesiastical offices, but his
heart was never in his profession ; he would
neither preach nor confess, and he devoted his
time to writing political pamphlets which were
saturated with the doctrines of the philosophical
school. These pamphlets attracted the notice of
the public, and one of them, which has remained,
made him famous. 'What is the Tiers État?'
asked Siéyes. 'Everything. What has it been
until now in the political order? Nothing.
What does it demand to become? Something.
There are 80,000 priests and 110,000 nobles in
this country ; there are from 25,000,000 to
26,000,000 of human beings in it ; judge for
yourselves what this implies.' Though a powerful writer, he was an indifferent speaker, and his
voice was seldom heard in the National Assembly
—as he was the first to style the States-General.
'The silence of Siéyes is a national calamity,'
said Mirabeau, who valued his gifts highly, but

who became jealous of Siéyes as soon as he noticed the effect his praise produced. 'See,' he exclaimed, 'since yesterday the shoulders of Siéyes are bent—he is overwhelmed. I have charged him with a load of fame he will never be able to bear.' Siéyes, however, concerned himself with reorganising the Government; he helped in creating the National Guard, promoted the reform of taxation, the division of France into departments, and the establishment of municipalities. In 1790 he refused the offer of a bishopric under the new Civil Constitution of the Clergy, and in the following year he joined a committee which had been appointed with the object of framing a new constitution, but soon was obliged to leave it, as he was unable to agree with his colleagues. His voice was heard again when he voted the King's death in the laconic but forcible words which have since been impugned, 'La mort sans phrase.' Though he kept in the background Siéyes was not idle, but as he feared to become a suspect, many of the proposals which emanated from his fertile brain were placed before the Convention not by himself, but through his friends. Robespierre, however, was not to be deceived. 'Citizens,' he said, 'this is not the work of those who are presenting it to you. I distrust its real author.' Being thus put on his guard, Siéyes thereafter remained in the shade, and so completely did he succeed in avoiding notoriety, that at the close of the Revolution he was asked what he had been doing during the Terror. 'I lived,' he replied. In November 1793 Siéyes had publicly abjured his priestly office. He may have been compelled to this act by fear, but it was consistent with his principles. 'Many years since,' he said on that occasion, 'I gave up my ecclesiastical character. But while my professions of faith are well known, I must be allowed to avail myself of this opportunity to say, and I will repeat it a hundred times if necessary, that the only worship I know is that of liberty and equality, and my only religion is that of humanity and my country.' At the same time he renounced the pension of 10,000 francs allowed him by the State in commutation of the income of his former benefice. After the fall of Robespierre he joined the Committee of Public Safety, but refused the presidency of the Convention, and he declined also to become a member of the Directory, though he joined the Council of Five Hundred. In 1798 he was appointed Minister Plenipotentiary to Berlin, and on his return assisted Bonaparte in planning the *coup d'état* of Brumaire, hoping perhaps to share his future honours. He was appointed one of the three Consuls, but held office for one day only, as he was unable to agree with, or unwilling to submit to, the future Emperor, who would not listen to his constitutional proposals. When Siéyes urged that a Grand Elector should be installed at

Versailles with an income of 5,000,000 francs, but that his only privilege should be the nomination of an Executive Council, Napoleon contemptuously inquired, 'Citizen Siéyes, what would this fattened pig do in the palace of Versailles?' An angry discussion followed, and Siéyes, seeing that he had been outwitted, turned to his friends and said, 'Now you have a master. He knows everything, he is capable of everything, and he does everything.' To conciliate Siéyes, or render him harmless, Napoleon, on taking the Imperial crown, made him President of the Senate and a Count, and endowed him handsomely.

On the Restoration he had to leave France, but he returned to Paris in 1830, and died there in 1836. He suffered from hallucinations in his old age, being haunted by the horrors of the past. 'If M. de Robespierre should call, please say I am out,' he said one day to his servant. Siéyes was deficient in character and enterprise. He cared more for his own personal safety than for the success of his many schemes. Fouché might be compared to a snake that coils itself round the trunk of a tree and glides up to its highest branches ; Siéyes to a mole that shuns the light of day and works laboriously underground, but only succeeds in throwing up ephemeral dust-heaps.

CONCLUSION

WITH the dissolution of the Convention in 1795 and the establishment of the Directory the Revolution virtually came to a close. It had changed from its original aim, the foundation of a constitutional monarchy, and slid rapidly down a steep incline into an abyss where its farther progress was arrested. That it deviated from its first ideal was greatly due to the rottenness and effeteness of the old order, which fell to pieces like a house of cards at the first gust of the popular whirlwind, and could neither control nor assist the National Assembly in its work of violent reform. The country having drifted into a state of complete anarchy, the National Assembly, which now re-named itself the Constituent Assembly, had been succeeded by the Legislative Assembly, and this again by the Convention, each body outrivalling its predecessor in the profession of advanced principles and the indulgence in arbitrary acts. The young and inexperienced men of the Convention, in their hatred of the old order and their enthusiasm for the new, could only meet the difficulties they encountered with blind force. Torn by internal feuds, they employed their energies and their time on wholesale destruction, in traducing and slaying each other. When nothing remained for the Convention to destroy, it quietly expired. Many Deputies belonged to the Commune and the Jacobin Club, and, dominated as they were by the Paris mob, the members of the Committee of Public Safety handed over their countrymen to a Lebon, a Carrier, a Fouquier-Tinville, not only to gratify their own thirst for vengeance and lust of blood, but to carry out the mandate of the electorate. By the force of circumstances a small band of energetic but sinister men rose to power, to whom the worst crimes of the Revolution were due. A grave responsibility rested on them, yet it may be said on their behalf that deeply as they sinned, they erred in the belief that they were serving their country.

When the Directory first met on 27th October 1795, confusion prevailed in every department of the Government and dissatisfaction was rife in the country. The Republic, it is true, was safe ; the Dauphin had just died in prison, the Princes of the Royal House were helpless and friendless exiles ; the democracy had established its claims, and its rights would never be infringed again—any more than the privileges of the nobility would be revived. Those of the old order who had not succumbed were outlaws or fugitives, their property had been confiscated or sold, their title-deeds had been reduced to ashes under the ruins of their châteaux, and the majority of them had forfeited the esteem of their country by enlisting against it under a foreign flag. From these there was nothing to fear. But the public exchequer was empty ; the assignats were worthless,[1] and it appeared as if the efforts the nation had made to gain its liberty and improve its condition had been worse than wasted.

Religious liberty had been proclaimed, but the promoters of religious toleration were rewarded for their liberality by the proscription of the Catholic faith, whose priests were hunted down like vermin. There was equality before the law, but the pioneers of freedom had been imprisoned and slaughtered. There was equality of taxation, but trade and commerce were depressed, and ruin stared the middle classes in the face, the classes who had rejoiced over the abolition of the guilds and the introduction of fiscal reforms. Famine stalked through the land, and the people who now owned the acres of their former lords were breadless, while the soldiers who had saved the Republic were ill-paid, ill-fed, ill-clothed, and sustained reverses which checked their victorious march. Time alone could unfold the beneficent results of the Revolution, of which France was as yet only dimly conscious. Perhaps the most important of these

---

[1] Over 38,000,000,000 of assignats had been issued.

results was her complete unification. Instead of being split up into autonomous provinces, each possessing a separate administration and organisation, special laws, different currencies and taxation, and protective duties—a system as harassing to private individuals as it was injurious to the State—France was now a homogeneous realm. The Vendée was still making spasmodic and heroic efforts on behalf of 'God and the King,' but they were extinguished within a few years. Soon all Frenchmen would be united in a common bond, animated by the same spirit, and working for the same cause, welded into one people, and developing the vast and unexplored resources of the land, not for the advantage of a limited and selfish class, but for that of the whole people.

But this satisfactory issue was still hidden by the veil of the future. The task of the Directory consisted in securing the issue and in lifting the veil. Of its five members, Carnot alone was a man of great capacity. Barras, though resolute and conciliatory, was a corrupt voluptuary, and La Revellière-Lépeaux, Rewbell, and Letourneur were merely honest, industrious, ordinary men of business. But they entered upon their work with energy and perseverance, and they were greatly assisted in fulfilling it by the apathy of the country, which, weary of disorder, only desired to be well governed. Paris, then as it always has been, the leader of French thought, political, initiative, and social ideas, set the fashion of supporting the Ministers who dispensed a semi-regal hospitality at the Luxembourg with Republican urbanity. The gloom which had long obscured the brilliant city was rapidly dispelled under an explosion of exuberant joy-fulness, with which the glee an invalid feels on recovering from a long and severe illness is feeble in comparison. For the first time for many years the inhabitants of Paris felt free. To meet after a long separation a beloved relative who was supposed to have perished restored happiness to many a household ; to sleep in one's home without the fear of a domi-ciliary visit was a new and grateful experience ; to indulge in the comforts of life after having been immured in prison, insulted by vile jailers, or stowed away in bare garrets or cellars, was a source of keen delight ; to talk politely and not be accused of being an aristocrat, to be once more an active citizen of this bright and beautiful world overjoyed every class of the population. The troubles and sorrows of the past were forgotten, and the cares of the future ignored. 'Bals des Victimes' were given for those who had lost relatives on the guillotine ; ladies indulged in the fantastic costume of Greek hetaires, young men wore the most extrava-gant dress ; gay crowds thronged the cafés, the shops, the gambling houses, and the gardens of the Palais Royal, where Camille Desmoulins but a few years before had delivered his harangues, invented a new combination of national colours, and distributed the newly invented tricoloured cockade among the people. Salons were opened in which Madame d'Houdetot, once the idol of Rousseau, Madame de Staël, and Josephine Beauharnais added the wit and polish of the old *régime* to the graces of Madame Tallien and Madame Récamier, and helped to soften the manner and tone of the vigorous but rough, new generation of men. While society was thus being reconstructed from the old and the new elements, it expanded into the gayest luxuriance, and confidence was quickly restored amongst the people at large. Financiers and speculators displayed an unusual activity; workmen and artisans after six years of rioting and idleness returned to their trades with renewed skill and ardour. To the clear-headed observer, however, it must have been plain that the Directory was but a makeshift, and the Constitution a transient meteor. It was not to be expected that the nation, having suffered such untold woes, and having submitted to such terrible ordeals, could long rest content with a Government, which, as a wag remarked, was like a work in five volumes, which were so flat that they could easily be bound into a thin book. But as yet the most sagacious politicians could not tell in what manner, and by whose energy the temporary condition of affairs would be efficiently dealt with and settled ; and they little imagined that the man lived in their midst by whose genius, within a decade, France would be raised above every nation on the Continent. 'Do you know who that is ? ' Barras asked Talma, the tragedian, at a reception, pointing out a young officer who was leaving the room. 'I only know that he is called Bonaparte, and has commanded the troops of the Convention,' answered the actor. ' Well,' added Barras, ' you have just seen the new General-in-Chief of the Army which is about to proceed to Italy.' Talma looked surprised, and Barras continued—' Yes, he is a young man full of vigour and promise, and great things are expected of him.'

THE END

Printed by R. & R. CLARK, LIMITED, *Edinburgh.*

Printed in the United States
20392LVS00004B/161